The Gun Digest Book of
FIREARMS ASSEMBLY/ DISASSEMBLY

PART VI
LAW ENFORCEMENT WEAPONS

by J.B. Wood

DBI Books, Inc., Northfield, Ill.

Editorial Staff:

Editor
  Harold A. Murtz
Graphic Design
  MacDonald Graphics
Cover Illustration
  James M. Triggs
Publisher
  Sheldon L. Factor

This book is dedicated to all of the professional law enforcement officers who each day put their lives on the line for our protection.

Acknowledgements

My thanks to these people, who helped to make this book possible: John S. Yarger, John A. Yarger, and James W. Yarger of Lock & Load Gun Shop, Mike Burkdoll, Bruce M. Louden, John Wright, Ed Marksberry, E. S. "Mac" Bowen II, Wesley Hampton, Bill Clede, Howard French and Jan Libourel of Guns & Ammo Magazine, Mitch Kalter of Action Arms, Dave Ecker and Charles Gara of Charter Arms, John Bressem of Heckler & Koch, Wayne Daniel of RPB Industries, Ira Trast of Auto-Ordnance, Col. Frank Pettway of Commando Arms, John R. Wilkinson of Wilkinson Arms, Paul Marlow and Wendy Markham of Detonics, Barry Kahn of FTL Marketing, Martin Mandall of Mandall Shooting Supplies, Rex Thomas of Browning, Andrew Papanek of Demro, and Russ Moure of Interarms.

A special Thanks to Jim Yeaman, without whom one entire section would have been much more difficult.

CONTENTS

INTRODUCTION

In the larger cities and metropolitan areas, police forces will usually have one or more officers who are designated as "Armorers" or "Weapon Maintenance Officers." As the terms indicate, it's their job to make minor repairs of the department's guns, or do extensive cleaning that requires total takedown and reassembly. An example of the latter might be a case in which an officer's gun was subjected to immersion in water or mud in the course of duty. In many departments, even some of those in smaller communities, the armorer-designates will have attended one of the annual seminars or brief schooling sesions provided by the major arms manufacturers or U.S. Government agencies.

In much smaller towns, the departments frequently can't spare a man to act as a full-time armorer, though some may be fortunate to have an officer who is also an arms hobbyist, and who can do some maintenance. For routine repair, thorough cleaning, and other general work, many of the smaller departments rely on gunsmiths or gunshops in their areas. While most gunsmiths will give police work priority, especially for individual officers, some are reluctant to take on quantity jobs for departments. Larger numbers of guns given priority will extend the waiting time of regular civilian customers, and payment by small cities and towns is often quite slow.

So, it's an advantage when individual officers can do simple maintenance of their own guns. The original instruction booklets furnished with the guns will help, up to a point, but none of these go beyond field-stripping. The same can be said of most of the "takedown" books that have been published, though some do go a bit further than the factory manuals, on some guns. This series of books is designed to help both the amateur and the professional, with clear photo-illustrated instructions for complete disassembly and reassembly.

The first five volumes of this series covered automatic pistols, revolvers, rimfire rifles, centerfire rifles, and shotguns, in that order. With the exception of two or three "duty weapons," an effort has been made to avoid duplication with information in the other books. For certain guns in police use which are not included in this book, the instructions can be found in the other volumes. For example, the Colt Trooper is in *Part II: Revolvers,* and the Ruger Mini-14 and the U.S. Carbine are covered in *Part IV: Centerfire Rifles*.

Some of the tools for proper takedown and maintenance are not obtainable from ordinary sources, so a tool section is included, with the addresses of firms supplying these special items.

Assuming a certain level of intelligence among my readers, I don't begin each set of instructions with the standard warning about emptying the gun, but I will say it once, right here: *Before taking any gun apart, be sure all cartridges are removed.* Don't rely on the feed and ejection systems—make an actual visual inspection. Also, guard your eyes against springs and spring-powered parts by wearing safety glasses.

A good companion to this book is the *Gun Digest Book of Exploded Firearms Drawings,* also available from DBI Books, Inc., showing parts relationships of more than 300 guns.

J. B. Wood
Raintree House
Corydon, Kentucky
April, 1981

A Note on Reassembly

Most of the firearms covered in this book can be reassembled by simply reversing the order of disassembly, carefully replacing the parts in the same manner they were removed. In a few instances, special instructions are required, and these are listed with each gun under "Reassembly Tips." In certain cases, reassembly photos are also provided.

If there are no special instructions or photos with a particular gun, you may assume that it can just be reassembled in reverse order. During disassembly, note the relationship of all parts and springs, and lay them out on the workbench in the order they were removed. By following this procedure you should have no difficulty.

TOOLS

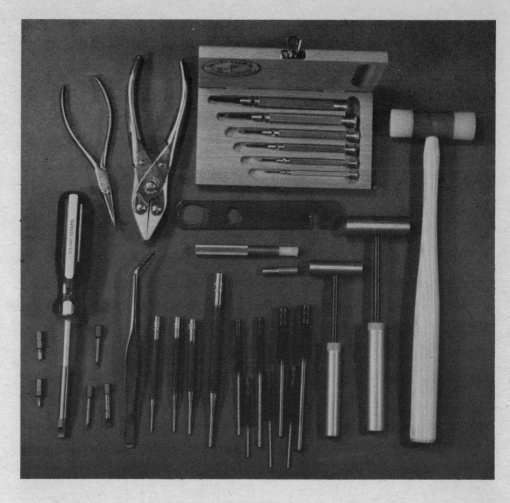

The tools shown here, and on the following pages, are absolutely the best for takedown and reassembly. Except for a few special-purpose and shop-made items, they are available from one of these sources:

Brownells
Route 2, Box 1
Montezuma, Iowa 50171

B-Square Company
P.O. Box 11281
Fort   Worth, Texas 76109

Chapman Manufacturing Company
Route 17
Durham, Connecticut 06422

General Instructions:

Screwdrivers: Always be sure the blade of the screwdriver **exactly** fits the slot in the screw head, both in thickness and in width. If you don't have one that fits, grind or file the tip until it does. You may ruin a few screwdrivers, but better them than the screws on a fine shotguns.

Slave pins: There are several references in this book to slave pins, and some non-gunsmith readers may not be familiar with the term. A slave pin is simply a short length of rod stock (in some cases, a section of a nail will do) which is used to keep two parts, or a part and a spring, together during reassembly. The slave pin must be very slightly smaller in diameter than the hole in the part, so it will push out easily as the original pin is driven in to retain the part. When making a slave pin, its length should be slightly less than the width of the part in which it is being used, and the ends of the pin should be rounded or beveled.

Sights: Nearly all dovetail-mounted sights are drifted out toward the right, using a nylon, aluminum, or brass drift punch.

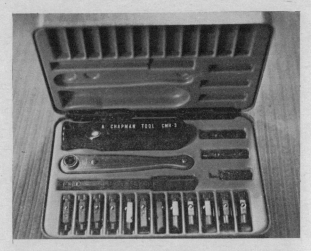

1. This screwdriver set from Chapman has 14 interchangeable bits in various sizes, and comes in a padded steel case that is pocket-size. It's designed specifically for gun work, and the quality is excellent. The price is $18.75.

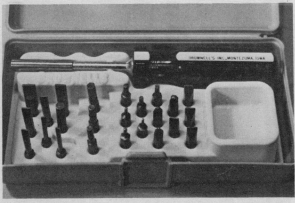

2. When a larger screwdriver is needed, this set from Brownells covers a wide range of blade sizes and also has Phillips- and Allen-type inserts. The tips are held in place by a strong magnet, yet are easily changed. These tips are very hard. With enough force you might manage to break one, but they'll never bend. Price of the complete set is about $21.

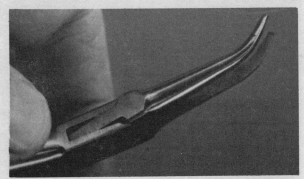

3. You should have at least one good pair of bent sharp-nosed pliers. These, from Brownells, have a box joint and smooth inner faces to help prevent marring. Price is about $8.

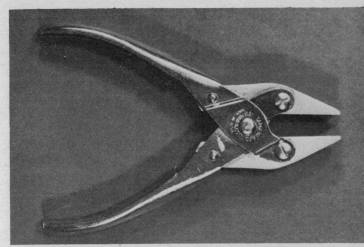

4. For heavier gripping, these Bernard parallel-jaw pliers from Brownells have smooth-faced jaw-pieces of unhardened steel to prevent marring of parts. Price is about $8.

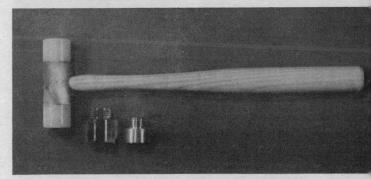

5. For situations where a non-marring rap is needed, this hammer from Brownells is ideal. It is shown with nylon faces on the head, but other faces of plastic and brass are also available. All are easily replaceable. Cost is about $8 with three faces.

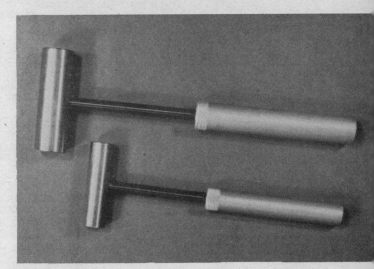

6. For drifting out pins, these small all-metal hammers from B-Square are the best I've seen. Two sizes (weights) are available and they're well worth the modest cost. About $15 for both.

7. For situations where reach and accessability are beyond the capabilities of sharp-nosed pliers, a pair of large sharp-nosed forceps (tweezers) will be invaluable. From Brownells, about $2.

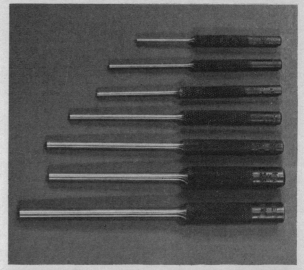

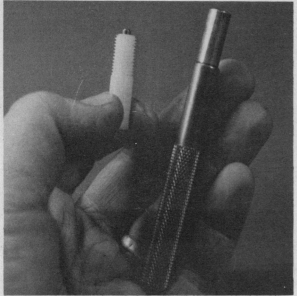

8. One of the most-used tools in my shop is this nylon-tipped drift punch, shown with an optional brass tip in place on the handle. It has a steel pin inside the nylon tip for strength. From Brownells, and absolutely essential. Price is about $2 for the set.

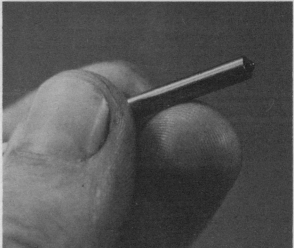

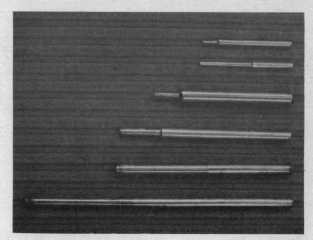

10. These punches by Mayhew are designed specifically for roll pins and have a projection at the center of the tip to fit the hollow center of a roll pin, driving it out without deformation of the ends. From Brownells, about $12 for the set.

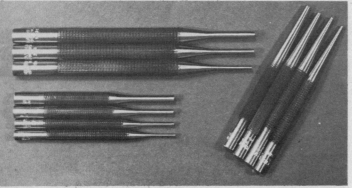

9. A good set of drift punches will prevent a lot of marred pins. These, from Brownells, are made by Mayhew. The tapered punches at the right are for starting pins, the others for pushing them through. Two sizes are available—4 inches (about 98¢ each) or 6 inches (about $1.25).

11. Some of the necessary tools are easily made in the shop. These non-marring drift punches were made from three sizes of welder's brazing rod.

12. This firing pin bushing spanner wrench from B-Square adjusts to fit all bushing holes, from $\frac{3}{16}''$ to $\frac{7}{16}''$ spacing. The pins are replaceable. About $35.00.

14. One of three stock wrenches from B-Square, this one is designed especially for use on the Remington Model 1100. About $22.00

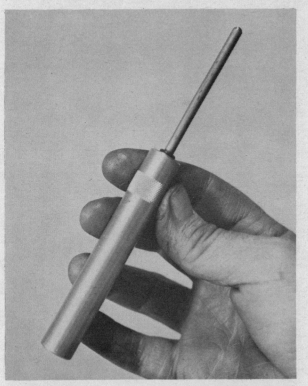

13. Designed to fit the Winchester Model 12, this fore-end cap nut wrench is also usable on several other slide-action shotguns. From Brownells, about $3.00.

15. Conceived by Gun Digest Associate Editor Bob Anderson for B-Square, this handy tool is designed for pushing out the trigger group retaining cross-pins in the Remington shotguns, and will work on several others. A rubber ring at the base of the shaft protects the side of the receiver. About $15.00.

16. Another of the B-Square stock wrenches, this short version is designed especially for the Remington Model 870, but will work on several other guns. About $22.00.

18. For re-staking the shell stops on several of the Remington shotguns, this heavy tool from B-Square makes an awkward job a simple operation. About $30.00

17. This wrench from B-Square is for easy removal of the deeply recessed fore-end cap nut on the Remington Model 870. About $25.00

SECTION 1

In large law enforcement organizations, departmental regulations will usually specify the type and caliber of handgun to be carried by the individual officer. When the guns are purchased by the department, or by the city, a particular manufacturer will usually be chosen to supply them. Up to the present time, the guns were sure to be double action revolvers in 38 Special chambering, but this is gradually changing. In smaller forces, with the guns often owned by each officer, there is sometimes more leeway in the choice of sidearms. The handguns covered in this section are those in most prevalent use by police agencies today.

DUTY SIDEARMS

CHARTER POLICE BULLDOG

Data:	Charter Police Bulldog
Origin:	United States
Manufacturer:	Charter Arms Corporation Stratford, Connecticut
Cartridge:	38 Special
Cylinder Capacity:	6 rounds
Over-all length:	9 inches
Barrel length:	4 inches
Weight:	21 ounces

Newly introduced at the time this was written, the Charter Police Bulldog is nearly a pound lighter than comparable police revolvers. The gun is also available in short barrel and heavy barrel models. Except for a revised ejector rod system, the gun is mechanically similar to all of the other Charter revolvers, and the instructions will apply generally to those as well.

Disassembly:

1. Remove the crane pivot screw at the lower front of the frame.

2. Operate the cylinder latch, and remove the crane and cylinder assembly toward the left.

3. Remove the crane and cylinder arbor unit toward the front.

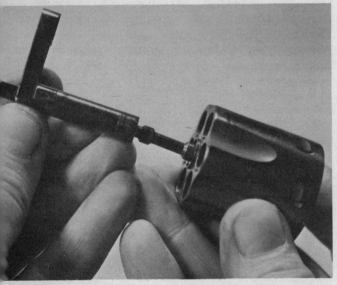

4. Push the ejector rod to move the ejector/ratchet out of the rear of the cylinder, and hold it there. Pull the ejector rod forward, and turn it until its internal cross-pin aligns with the cross-hole in the shaft of the ejector/ratchet piece. Use a very small drift punch to push out the cross-pin. **Caution:** *Removal of the drift punch after the pin is out will release the ejector rod toward the front, and the internal retaining sleeve toward the rear, so control both. Take care not to lose the tiny retaining pin.*

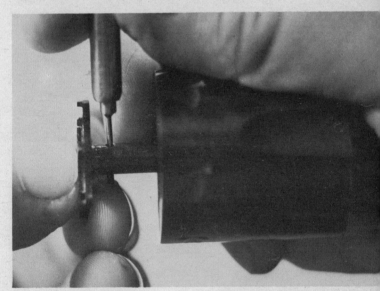

5. Remove the retaining sleeve and locking spring from the rear of the ejector/ratchet.

6. Remove the ejector rod and ejector return spring from the front of the cylinder. When removing the spring from the rod, take care not to lose the compression washer.

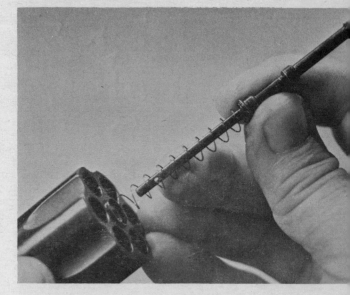

7. Remove the ejector/ratchet from the rear of the cylinder.

8. Move the cylinder latch to the rear and cock the hammer. Insert an opened paper clip or some other small tool through the cross-hole in the hammer strut. Lower the hammer gently, and the hammer spring system will be trapped as a unit.

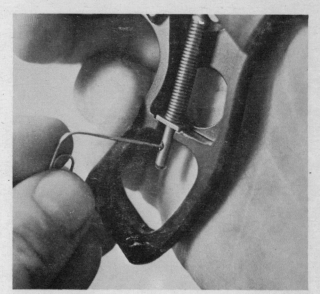

9. Remove the trapped mainspring unit downward and toward the left. The unit can be disassembled by gripping the upper knob and pressing the base plate against a slightly opened vise, then withdrawing the clip. Control the compressed spring.

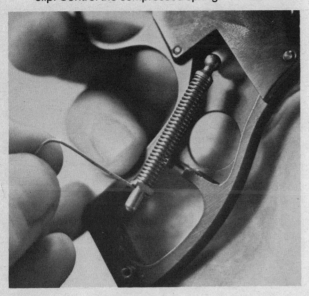

10. Remove the hammer pivot screw.

11. Move the cylinder latch toward the rear, pull the trigger, and remove the hammer from the top of the frame. Removal of the small cross-pin at the front of the hammer will release the double action lever and its plunger and spring.

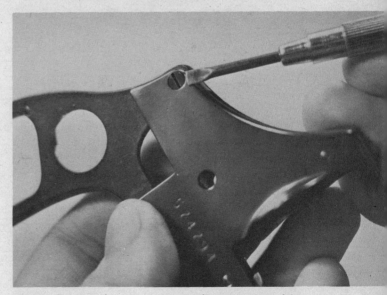

12. Remove the cross-screw at the upper rear of the frame.

13. Drift out the front sub-frame cross-pin toward the right.

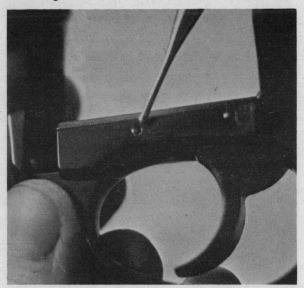

14. Drift out the rear sub-frame cross-pin toward the right.

15. Remove the sub-frame downward.

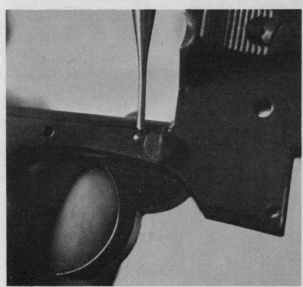

16. Restrain the trigger, and drift out the trigger cross-pin toward the right.

17. Remove the trigger assembly downward. The transfer bar and cylinder hand are easily detached from each side of the trigger.

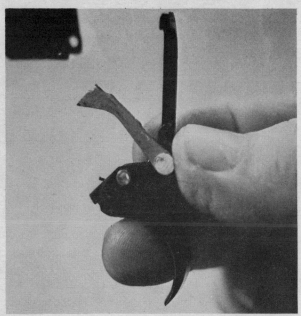

18. Push out the trigger pivot bushing, and remove the trigger spring upward.

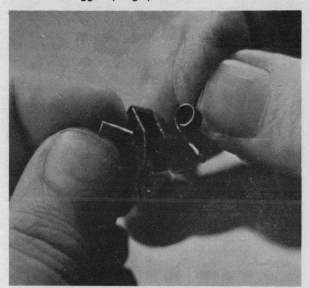

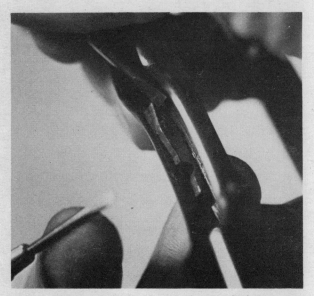

19. Depress the cylinder stop plunger, tip the stop out of its slot in the frame, and move it inward off its post for removal.

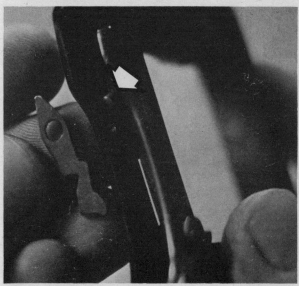

20. Remove the cylinder stop from the bottom of the frame. Take care to release the plunger and spring (arrow) slowly, and remove them from their well.

21. Remove the cylinder latch screw.

22. Remove the cylinder latch thumbpiece screw, and take care that the oblong cover plate and the plunger and spring are not lost.

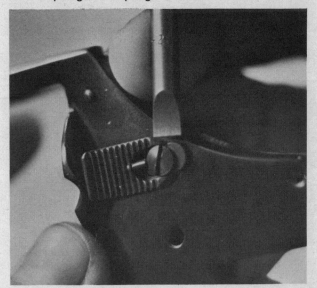

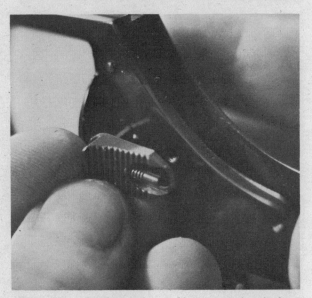

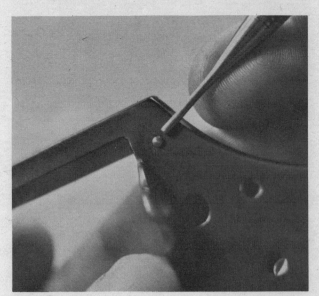

23. Move the thumbpiece to the rear to clear its front inner projection, and remove the thumbpiece toward the left. Remove the plunger and spring from the thumbpiece.

24. Drift out the cross-pin at the top of the frame toward the right, and remove the firing pin and its return spring toward the rear.

Reassembly Tips:

1. When replacing the thumbpiece, take care that the spring plunger bears on the edge of the thumbpiece screw, and is not trapped beneath it.

2. Use a small screwdriver to keep the plunger aligned as the screw is turned into place. Be sure the cover plate is properly positioned, with its long tab toward the rear, and take care that the unthreaded shaft of the screw passes through the hole in the plate.

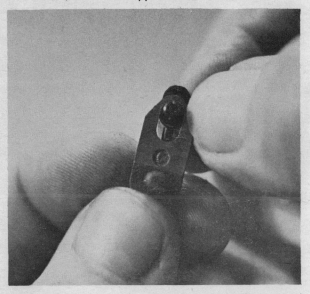

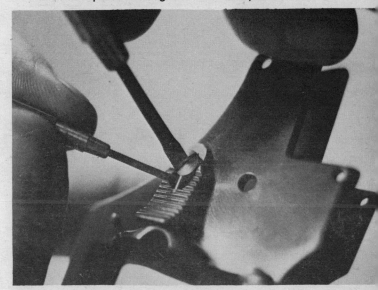

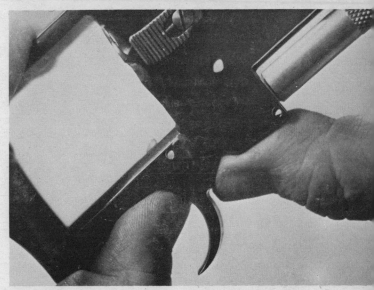

3. When installing the trigger assembly, note that the looped end of the spring must bear on the shelf of the cylinder hand at the rear. Place the trigger at the rear of the frame recess, with the upper arm of the spring bearing against the vertical inner surface of the frame. Keeping upward pressure on the trigger, move it forward, compressing the spring, and insert a drift punch to hold it in place while inserting the cross-pin.

4. The trigger can be moved into place more easily if a non-marring tool, such as a nylon-tipped drift punch, is used to push it forward.

5. Use a small-diameter tapered drift punch to depress the retaining sleeve while partially inserting the tiny cross-pin. Take care that the pin is not dislodged while inserting the ejector rod.

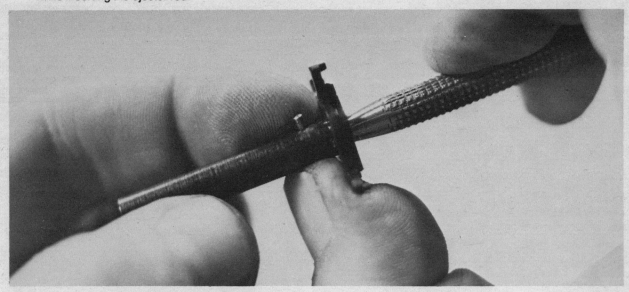

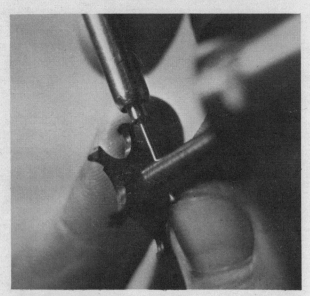

6. When the ejector rod is aligned, insert a very small drift punch to hold it in place while the retaining pin is pushed into place.

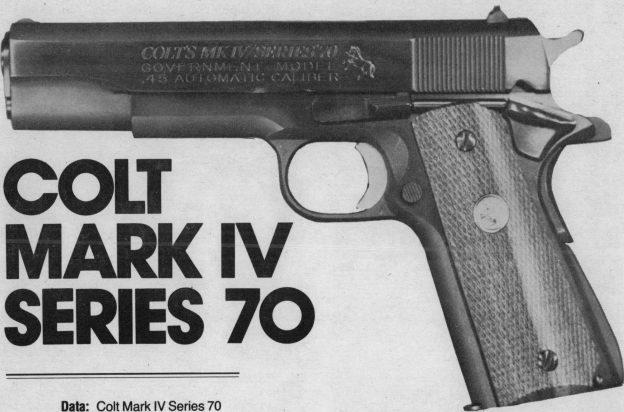

COLT MARK IV SERIES 70

Data:	Colt Mark IV Series 70
Origin:	United States
Manufacturer:	Colt Firearms Hartford, Connecticut
Cartridges:	45 ACP, 38 Super, 9mm Luger
Magazine Capacity:	45—7 rounds 38/9mm—9 rounds
Over-all length:	8⅜ inches (Commander—8 inches)
Height:	5⅜ inches
Barrel length:	5 inches (Commander— 4¼ inches)
Weight:	40 ounces (Commander— 36 ounces)

The current-production Mark IV Series 70 pistol differs only slightly from our standard Model 1911 service pistol and the shorter Commander version, and the instructions will apply to these as well. This is also true of several other commercial guns based on the Model 1911 pattern, such as the AMT Hardballer and the Vega.

Disassembly:

1. Remove the magazine and let the hammer down to fired position. Depress the checkered button below the barrel at the muzzle, and turn the barrel bushing toward the right side, while restraining the spring plug. **Caution:** *The recoil spring is under tension, so keep strong pressure on the checkered end of the plug, and ease it out when the bushing clears it.* On some guns, especially the current production types with the barrel-gripping bushing, it may be necessary to use a special wrench to turn the bushing.

2. Remove the plug from the end of the recoil spring. In some cases, it may be locked on the spring by an internal tab, and a slight turn will be necessary to free it.

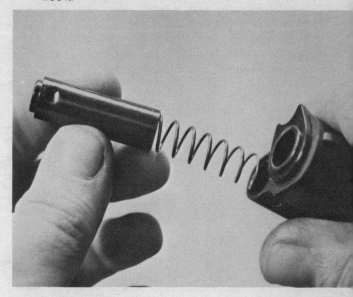

3. Cock the hammer, and move the slide back until the small semi-circular cut in its lower edge is aligned with the top rear of the slide stop.

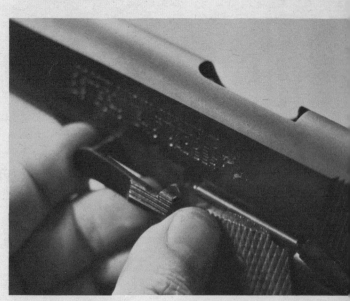

4. Push the right end of the slide stop shaft toward the left, and remove the slide stop from the left side.

5. Move the slide and barrel assembly forward off the frame.

6. Remove the recoil spring and its guide from the underside of the slide.

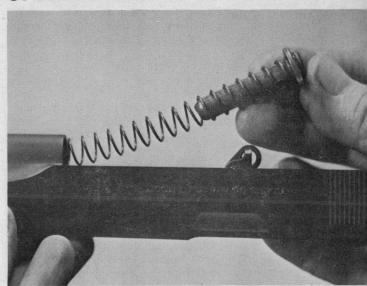

7. Rotate the barrel bushing toward the left side of the slide, aligning its lug with the lower front opening, and remove the bushing toward the front.

8. Tip the barrel link over forward, to allow clearance through the recoil spring tunnel. Move the barrel out the front of the slide.

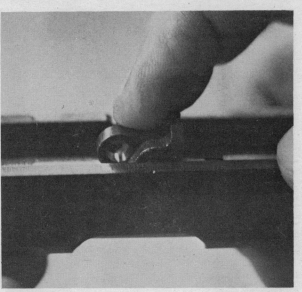

9. Depress the firing pin and slide the retainer downward for removal. **Caution:** *During removal of the retainer, restrain the firing pin against the tension of its return spring.*

10. Release the spring tension slowly, and remove the firing pin and its spring toward the rear.

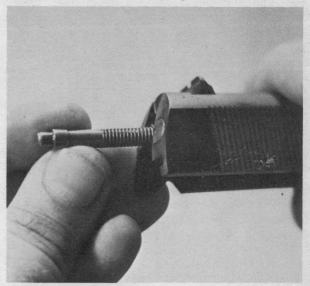

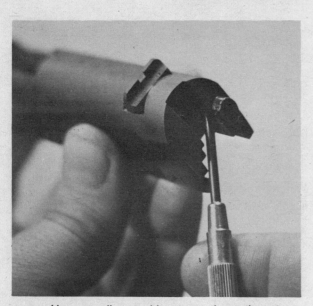

11. Use a small screwdriver to gently pry the extractor out toward the rear.

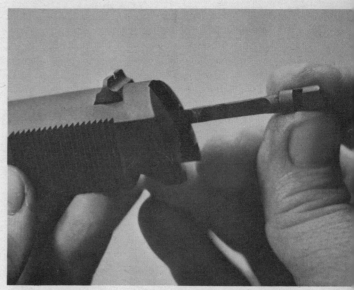

12. Remove the extractor toward the rear. The rear sight can be drifted out of its dovetail toward the right.

13. The mainspring housing retaining pin is located at the lower rear of the grip frame. With the hammer in fired position, drift out the mainspring housing retaining pin.

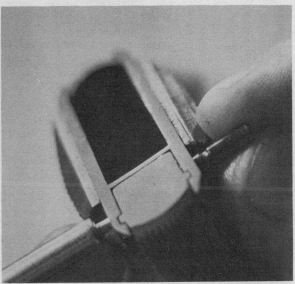

14. Slide the mainspring housing downward out of the grip frame. If the housing is tight, cocking the hammer will help to push it out.

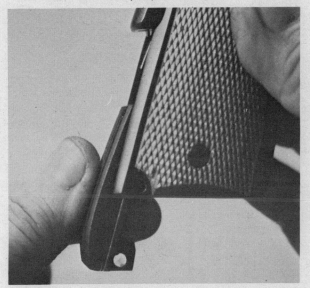

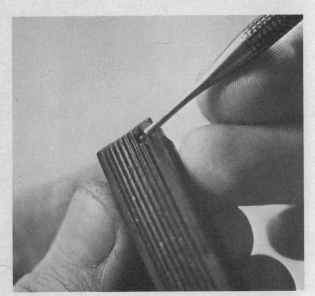

15. If necessary, the mainspring and its plungers can be removed from the housing by drifting out a small pin on the right near the top of the housing. The pin must be drifted inward. **Caution:** *This is a heavy spring, and it is under tension.* Insert a tool from the top to restrain it while pushing out the pin.

16. Cock the hammer, and move the safety toward the on-safe position while exerting slight pressure toward the left (pulling it out). When the internal projection of the safety aligns with its exit cut in the frame, the safety can be removed toward the left.

17. Remove the grip safety toward the rear.

18. Remove the combination spring toward the rear.

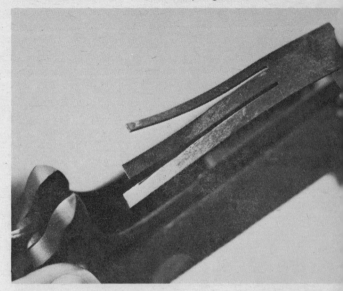

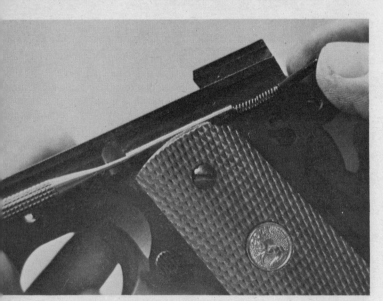

19. Use a small drift punch to push the slide stop plunger toward the rear, and remove the safety plunger, slide stop plunger, and their common spring toward the rear. The housing for these parts is mounted on the side of the frame by two internal projections, riveted in place, and removal and replacement should not be attempted without special tools.

20. Remove the hammer pivot pin toward the left.

21. Remove the hammer toward the rear.

22. The hammer strut can be removed by drifting out the small cross-pin at the lower rear of the hammer.

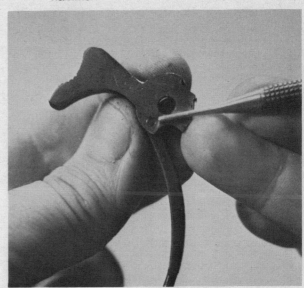

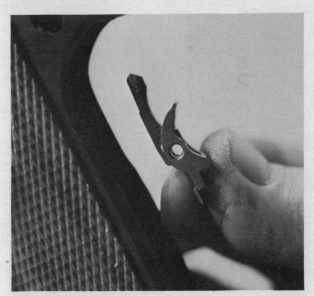

23. Remove the sear/disconnector pin toward the left.

24. Move the sear and disconnector downward, then out the rear of the frame. Note their relationship to aid reassembly.

25. Engage a small screwdriver in the slotted head of the magazine catch retainer, and depress the magazine catch until the retainer can be turned to the left (counter-clockwise) until it stops.

26. Remove the magazine catch assembly toward the right. Turning the retainer back toward the right will free the retainer and magazine catch spring for removal. The spring is under tension, so control it during removal.

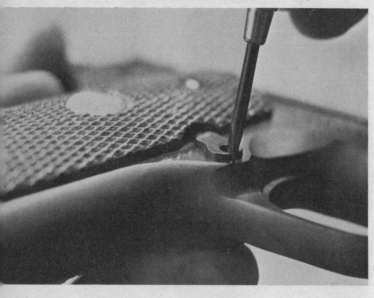

Reassembly Tips:

When installing the combination spring, be sure its left upper extension contacts the sear. When the spring is in place, slide the mainspring housing partially into the frame to hold the spring while installing the safety and grip safety.

When replacing the slide stop, look through the hole in the frame and be sure the barrel link is in position, in alignment with the hole, before inserting the slide stop. Moving the slide slightly will edge the link into place. Don't try aligning the link and the semi-circular clearance cut in the lower edge of the slide at the same time. Put the slide stop shaft through the link, then swing the stop up and align it with the clearance cut.

27. Remove the trigger toward the rear.

COLT POLICE POSITIVE

Data:	Colt Police Positive
Origin:	United States
Manufacturer:	Colt Firearms Hartford, Connecticut
Cartridge:	38 Special
Cylinder Capacity:	6 rounds
Over-all length:	8¾ inches
Barrel length:	4 inches
Weight:	23 ounces

The Police Positive was introduced in 1905, and the 38 Special chambering came along in 1907. During its many years of production, there were some slight changes in the external design, and in more recent times there were a few internal changes, mainly in the ejector system and the crane retainer. By 1973, when it was finally dropped from the Colt line, it had evolved into the gun shown here. For many departments, it is still the standard sidearm.

Disassembly:

1. Remove the crane retainer cap screw and its spring and plunger.

2. Operate the cylinder latch, open the cylinder, and position the cylinder so one of the chamber flutes is aligned with the frame shoulder at the front. Remove the cylinder and crane assembly toward the front.

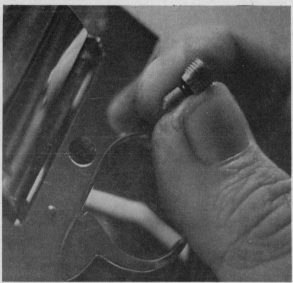

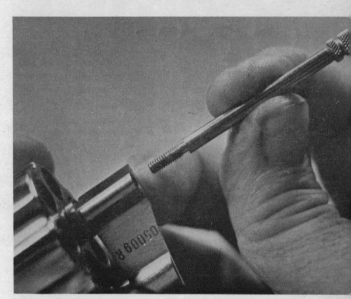

3. Grip the ejector rod knob with leather-padded pliers, and unscrew the rod, counter-clockwise (front view).

4. Remove the ejector rod toward the front.

5. Remove the crane toward the front.

6. Using the standard Colt tool from Brownells, unscrew the ejector spring retaining nut from inside the cylinder arbor on the crane. If the tool is unavailable, the nut can be removed from this late type gun by using a screwdriver of proper dimensions. Restrain the nut as it nears the end of its threads, as the ejector spring will be released.

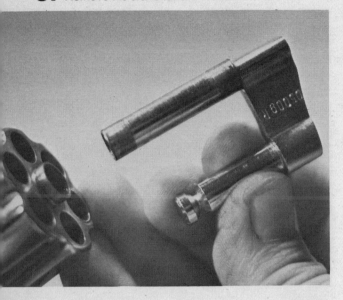

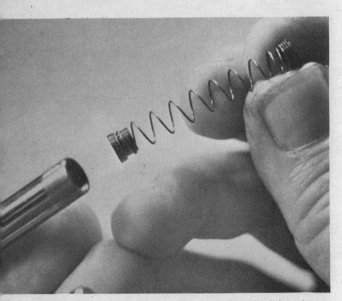

7. Remove the nut, the ejector spring, and the ejector rod bushing from the cylinder arbor.

8. Remove the ejector/ratchet from the rear of the cylinder.

9. Remove the grips, and take out the two sideplate screws on the left side.

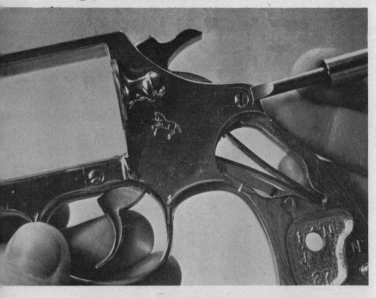

10. Hold the gun with the plate over the hand, and tap the grip frame with a nylon hammer. The sideplate will drop into the palm of the hand.

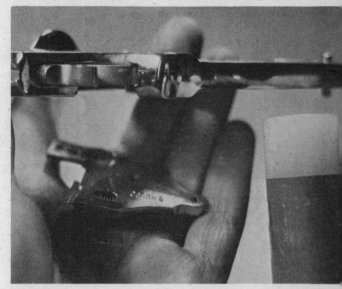

11. Remove the cylinder latch thumbpiece from the sideplate, and take out its spring.

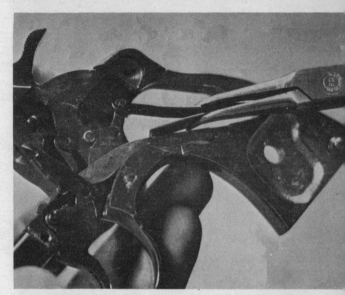

12. Push the mainspring out toward the left, compress it, and disengage its upper hooks from the hammer stirrup. Remove the spring toward the left.

13. Remove the cylinder hand toward the left.

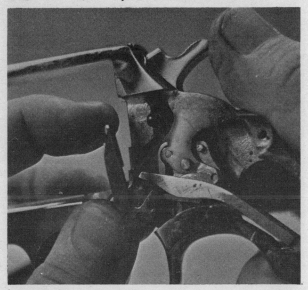

14. Drift out the rebound lever pivot pin.

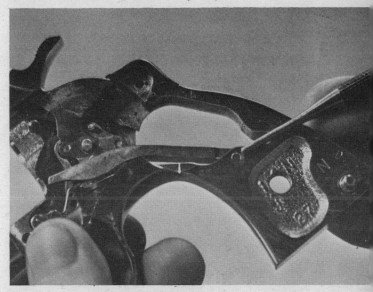

15. Move the rear end of the rebound lever upward, out of its recess in the grip frame, and remove the lever toward the left.

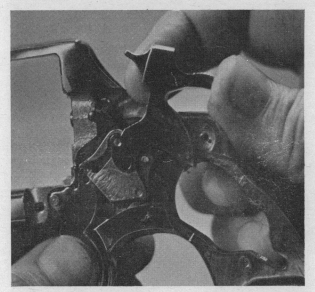

16. Tip the hammer back, and remove it toward the left. Removal of the cross-pin at the front of the hammer will release the double action lever and its spring. A cross-pin at the rear retains the spring stirrup. The firing pin is also retained by a cross-pin, riveted in place, and this should not be removed execpt for repair.

17. With the trigger in forward position, remove the cylinder latch plunger toward the rear.

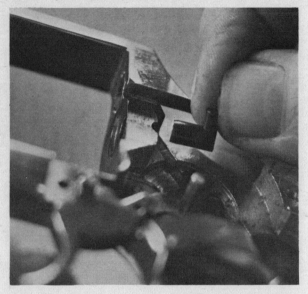

18. Pull the trigger to the rear, then move it to the left off its post. The hammer block safety and its flat lever will come out with the trigger.

19. The hammer block lever is easily removed from the trigger by sliding it forward to bring the larger opening in its slot even with the post on the trigger. The hammer block is separated from the lever in the same way.

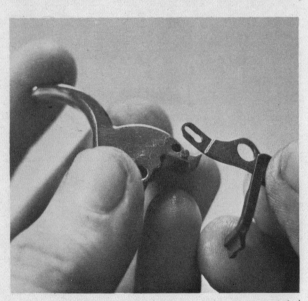

20. The cylinder stop and its spring are retained inside the right wall of the frame by a stepped pivot screw. After the screw is removed, tip the lower end of the spring out of its recess in the frame, and move the cylinder stop downward and toward the rear for removal.

Reassembly Tips:

1. When replacing the mainspring, engage the upper hooks with the stirrup on the hammer, set the lower arm of the spring on the rebound lever, and compress the spring as it is swung over into position. This can usually be done without tools.

2. When replacing the sideplate, hold the cylinder latch thumbpiece with its front edge even with the front edge of the sideplate. Be sure the cylinder latch plunger is in full forward position as the plate is moved into place.

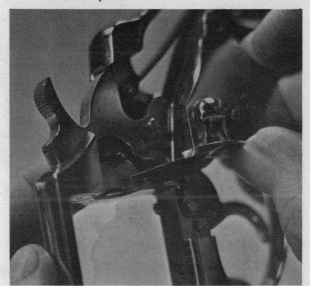

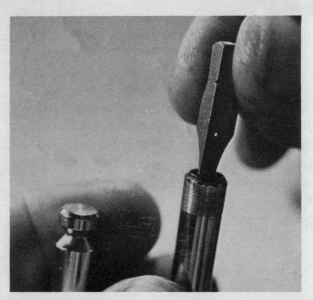

3. As noted in Disassembly Step #6, a screwdriver can be used to replace the ejector spring nut. Take care not to over-tighten it, as the fine threads are easily stripped.

RUGER POLICE SERVICE SIX

Data:	Ruger Police Service Six
Origin:	United States
Manufacturer:	Sturm, Ruger & Company Southport, Connecticut
Cartridge:	357 Magnum
Cylinder Capacity:	6 rounds
Over-all length:	9¼ inches
Barrel length:	4 inches
Weight:	33½ ounces

In addition to the "standard" four-inch barrel, the Police Service Six is also available with a short 2¾-inch barrel and a heavy four-inch version. There are actually three sub-models of the Police Service Six: The Model 107 in 357 Magnum, the Model 108 in 38 Special, and the Model 109 in 9mm Luger. Through all of these, the basic mechanism is the same, and the instructions will apply.

Disassembly:

1. Back out the grip screw, and remove the grips from the frame. A disassembly pin is stored inside the left grip. When removing the grip, take care that the pin is not lost.

2. Cock the hammer, and insert the disassembly pin through the transverse hole in the lower tip of the hammer strut.

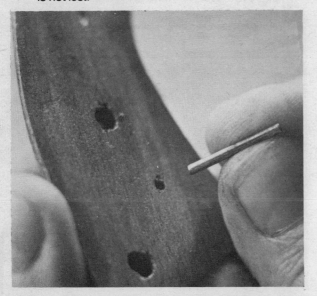

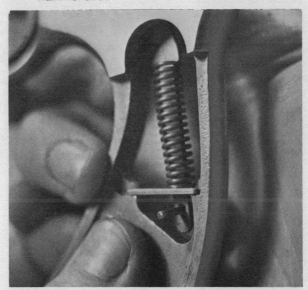

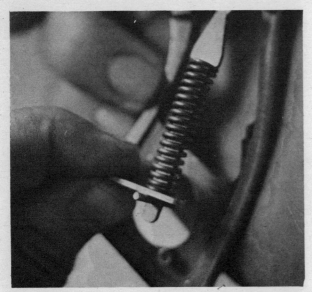

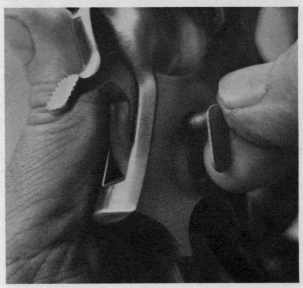

3. Let the hammer down slowly. The pin will come to rest against the compression plate, trapping the hammer spring on the strut. Remove the spring system toward the side and downward. If necessary, the spring unit can be disassembled by gripping the top of the strut and pushing the plate against a slightly opened vise while the pin is removed. **Caution:** *Control the spring.*

4. Push the hammer pivot toward the right until its tab can be grasped, and remove the hammer pivot toward the right.

5. Pull the trigger to the rear, and remove the hammer from the top of the frame. Drifting out the cross-pin at the front of the hammer will release the double action lever and its plunger and spring for removal toward the front.

6. Through the hammer opening in the top of the frame, the plunger which retains the trigger guard can be seen at the rear of the guard. Insert a screwdriver to lever the plunger toward the front, allowing the guard to move downward at the rear.

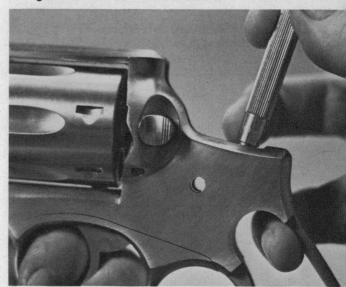

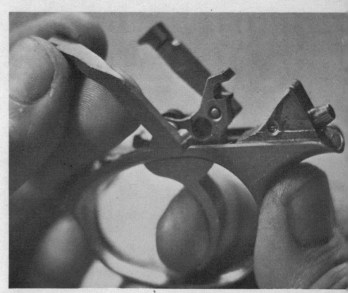

7. Tip the guard assembly down at the rear, move it toward the rear to clear its front lip, and remove it downward.

8. Pull the trigger slightly toward the rear, and remove the transfer bar toward the left.

9. Push out the trigger pin toward either side.

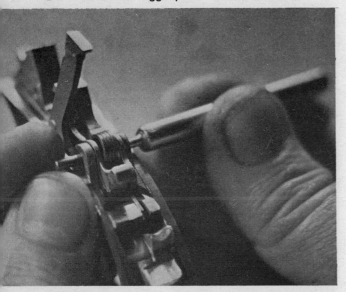

10. Remove the trigger assembly upward.

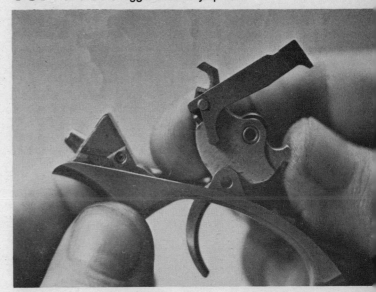

11. Restrain the cylinder hand plunger and spring, and remove the cylinder hand toward the right. Take out the plunger and spring toward the rear.

12. Removal of the pivot bushing will release the trigger spring. This should be done only if necessary for repair, and a roll pin punch should be used, to avoid damage to the bushing. The guard retaining plunger and spring are retained by a small roll pin. If these parts are to be removed, control the strong spring.

13. Removal of the guard unit will free the crane assembly to be taken off toward the front.

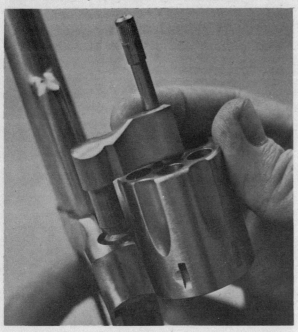

14. The cylinder stop plunger and spring can be removed from the rear of the crane pivot if necessary. They are held in place by a larger loop at the end of the spring, and can be pulled out to the rear. If the plunger detaches from the spring, the spring can be extracted by using a bent paper clip.

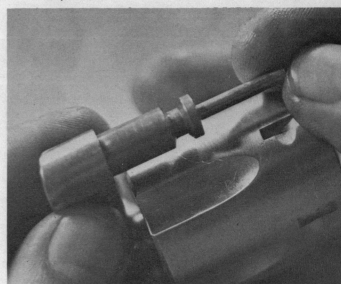

15. Grip the ejector rod knob with leather-padded smooth-jawed pliers, and unscrew the rod *clockwise* (front view). Note that this is a reverse thread. If the rod is very tight, grip the end of the rod in a leather-padded vise, insert two empty cartridge cases in opposed chambers, and turn the cylinder to free it.

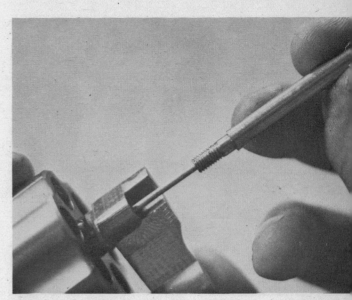

16. Remove the ejector rod toward the front.

17. Remove the center pin and its spring toward the front.

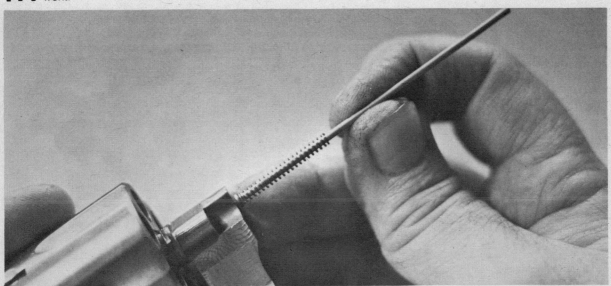

18. Remove the crane toward the front. Note that the small ball-bearing in the side of the arbor is staked in place, and removal is not advisable.

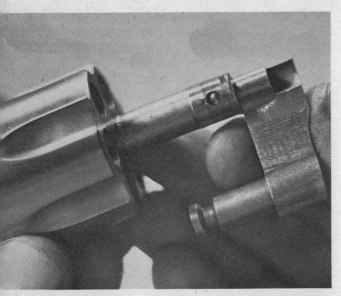

19. The small washer which compresses the ejector spring may stay inside the cylinder arbor when the crane is removed. Tap the arbor on the workbench to shake it out, and take care that it isn't lost.

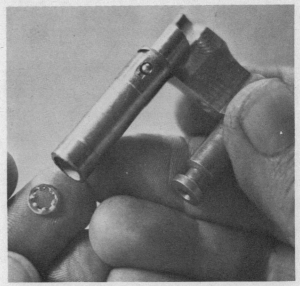

20. Remove the ejector spring from the front of the cylinder.

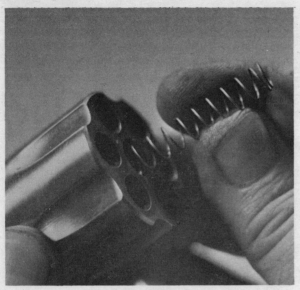

21. Remove the ejector/ratchet unit from the rear of the cylinder.

22. With the front tip of the center pin, push the cylinder lock pin out of the ejector shaft.

23. Remove the cylinder stop from the underside of the frame.

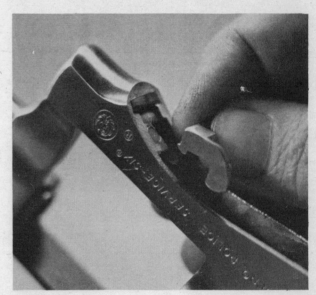

24. Use a small screwdriver to remove the vertical screw that retains the cylinder latch.

25. Insert a tool at the rear to push the inner projection of the cylinder latch rearward, then move it downward and toward the left.

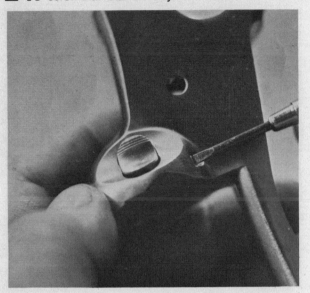

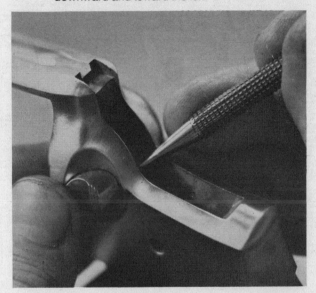

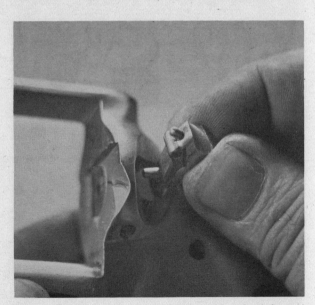

26. Remove the cylinder latch toward the left, and take out the plunger and spring mounted in the latch piece.

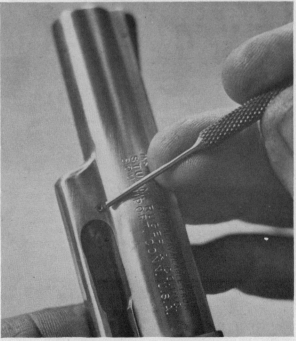

27. A small roll cross-pin in the ejector shroud retains the front latch plunger and its spring. When the pin is out, these parts are removed toward the rear. The front sight is also retained by a roll cross-pin.

Reassembly Tips:

28. The firing pin housing, firing pin, and return spring are retained in the frame by a cross-pin. The ends of this pin are contoured to match the curve of the frame, and removal will inevitably cause some deformation of the ends of the pin. Unless removal is necessary for repair, this system should not be disturbed. If it must be taken out, drift out the cross-pin and take out the firing pin assembly toward the front.

1. When replacing the trigger guard assembly in the frame, insert a tool at the rear to bear against the cylinder hand, keeping it pushed toward the right as the guard is snapped into place. If this is not done, the rear lobe of the hand may bind on the edge of its channel.

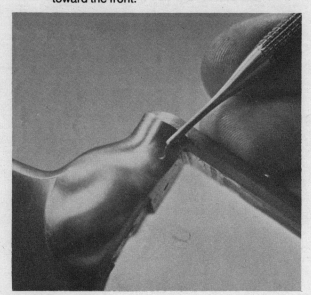

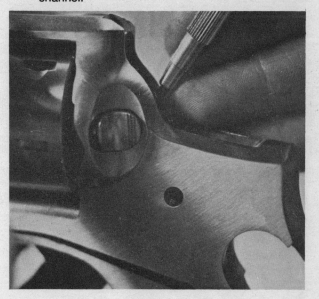

When replacing the cylinder latch in the frame, be sure the nose of the latch is visible in its hole at the center of the breech face before installing the screw.

When replacing the ejector rod, remember that it must be turned into place *counter-clockwise* (front view).

When replacing the cylinder lock pin in the ejector shaft, note that its collared end goes toward the front.

Before replacing the crane in the cylinder, be sure the ejector spring washer is inserted into the arbor.

When replacing the hammer spring unit, note that the longer tab of the base plate goes toward the front of the grip frame.

SMITH & WESSON MODEL 19

Data:	Smith & Wesson Model 19
Origin:	United States
Manufacturer:	Smith & Wesson Springfield, Massachusetts
Cartridge:	357 Magnum
Cylinder capacity:	6 rounds
Over-all length:	9½ inches (with 4-inch barrel)
Barrel lengths:	2½, 4, and 6 inches
Weight:	35 ounces

Although many police still carry the venerable Model 10 in 38 Special or the larger N-frame guns in 357 Magnum, many officers of my acquaintance have gone to the lighter Model 19, which first appeared on the scene around 1956. With its K-frame size and 357 Magnum chambering, the Model 19 is an ideal police revolver. Its stainless steel counterpart is the Model 66, which is otherwise identical.

Disassembly:

1. Remove the front sideplate screw, located on the right side, just forward of the trigger.

2. Operate the cylinder latch, open the cylinder, and remove the crane and cylinder assembly toward the front.

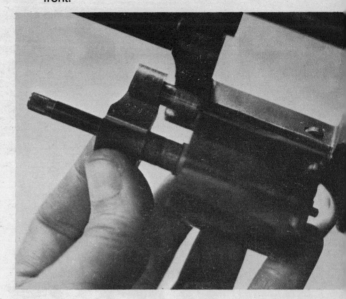

3. Remove the crane from the front of the cylinder. Grip the head of the ejector rod with leather-padded smooth-jawed pliers, and unscrew the rod *clockwise* (front view). Note that this is a reverse thread. If the rod is very tight, clamp the head of the rod in a padded vise, insert empty cartridge cases in two opposed chambers, and turn the cylinder to free the rod.

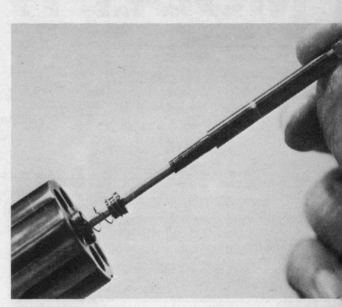

4. Remove the ejector rod toward the front.

5. Remove the center pin and its spring from the front of the cylinder.

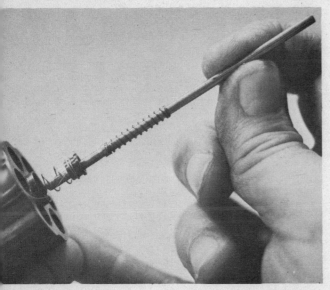

6. Remove the ejector spring and its bushing from the front of the cylinder.

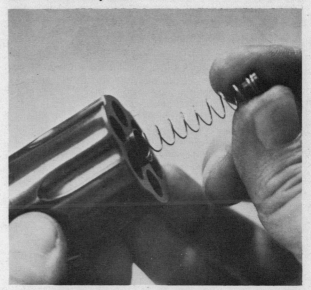

7. Remove the ejector/ratchet unit from the rear of the cylinder.

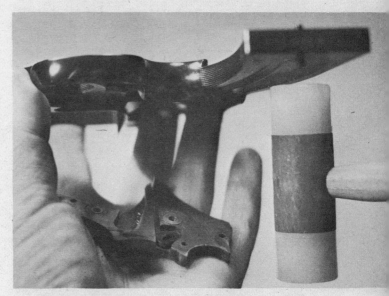

8. Remove the grips, and take out the two remaining sideplate screws on the right side. Hold the gun with the right side toward the palm of the hand, as shown, and tap the grip frame with a nylon hammer until the plate falls into the hand. The hammer block will likely come off with the sideplate, and it is easily lifted out of its recess in the sideplate.

9. Back out or remove the hammer spring strain screw, located at the lower front of the grip frame.

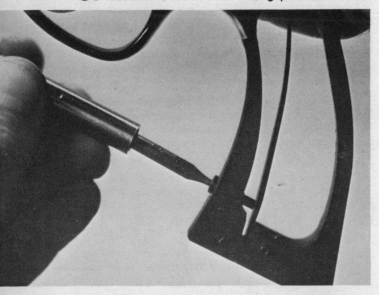

10. Disengage the spring hooks from the hammer stirrup, moving the hammer spring out of its recess in the grip frame, and remove the spring downward.

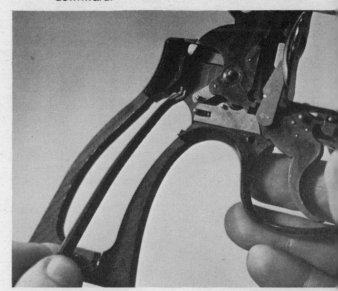

11. Hold the cylinder latch to the rear and pull the trigger to tip the hammer back. While holding the trigger to the rear, remove the hammer toward the right. Drifting out the small cross-pin at the front of the hammer will release the double action lever and its spring for removal. The small cross-pin at the lower rear of the hammer retains the stirrup. The firing pin is retained by a cross-pin which is riveted into coned areas on each side of the hammer, and should not be removed except for repair.

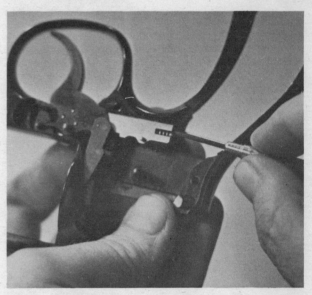

12. Insert a small screwdriver at the rear of the rebound slide and lift the rear of the slide off its base-post in the frame. The spring will be trapped on the shaft of the screwdriver. Remove the rebound slide and its spring.

13. Tip the cylinder hand to the rear to clear its slot in the frame, and remove the trigger toward the right.

14. Remove the cylinder hand from the right side of the trigger.

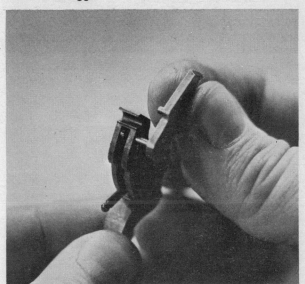

15. Drifting out the small cross-pin at the upper rear of the trigger will release the cylinder hand spring for removal. The lower pin retains the trigger strut. The front pin is a bearing for the hand spring, and need not be removed, as it retains no part.

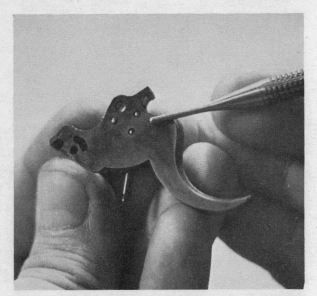

16. Depress the cylinder stop below its slot in the frame, and use a small screwdriver to nudge it out toward the right. When the spring mounted at its lower front nears the edge of the recess, control the spring, and ease it out.

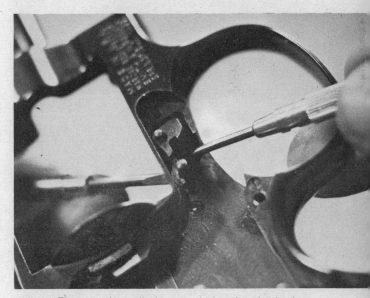

17. The trigger stop is retained by a small screw which also governs its adjustment. In normal takedown this should not be disturbed. If it is removed, it will require adjustment when re-installed.

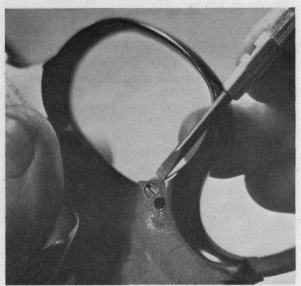

18. Remove the screw-slotted cap nut that retains the cylinder latch thumb-piece, and take off the thumb-piece toward the left.

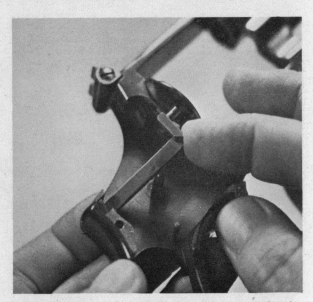

19. Move the cylinder latch toward the rear to clear its front post from its hole in the frame, tip the front outward, and remove the latch toward the right. Restrain the small plunger and spring at the rear during removal to prevent their escape.

20. Drifting out the small cross-pin at the front of the ejector shroud will release the front latch plunger and its spring for removal toward the rear.

Reassembly Tips:

21. The rear sight is retained by a small screw near its forward end, on top of the frame. Remove the screw, then slide the sight toward the rear and take it off. Disassembly of the sight is not recommended.

1. When replacing the cylinder hand on the trigger, insert a small tool at the rear of the trigger to lift the rear arm of the cylinder hand spring, and be sure that it is engaged with the top of the smaller internal pin on the hand.

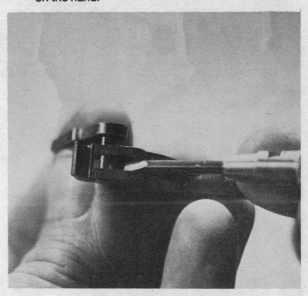

2. The internal parts are shown in their proper position before replacement of the sideplate.

3. When replacing the sideplate, be sure the hammer block is in its uppermost position, as shown in the previous step. Align the upper edge of the sideplate so the track on the inside of the plate encloses the top of the hammer block, then insert the upper lip of the plate and move the lower portion into place.

When replacing the ejector rod, remember that it must be turned into place *counter-clockwise* (front view). Screw it in snugly, but avoid over-tightening.

SMITH & WESSON MODEL 459

Data: Smith & Wesson Model 459

Origin: Smith & Wesson Springfield, Massachusetts

Cartridge: 9mm Luger

Magazine capacity: 14 rounds

Over-all length: 7⁷⁄₁₆ inches

Height: 5¹¹⁄₁₆ inches

Barrel length: 4 inches

Weight: 28 ounces

Except for the fully adjustable rear sight in its protective mount, the new Models 459 and 439 pistols look very much like the Models 59 and 39 which they replaced. Inside, though, there were extensive mechanical changes which make the takedown and reassembly very different in some areas. One of the most notable additions is an automatic firing pin block safety system.

Disassembly:

1. Remove the magazine and cock the hammer. Move the slide toward the rear until the slide latch notch in its lower edge is aligned with the pivot of the slide latch, and hold it there.

2. Use a non-marring tool to push the right tip of the slide latch cross-piece toward the left.

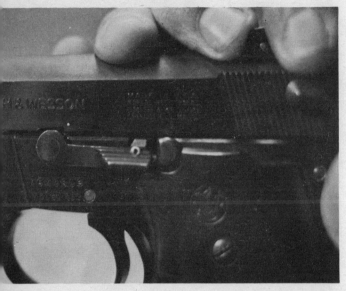

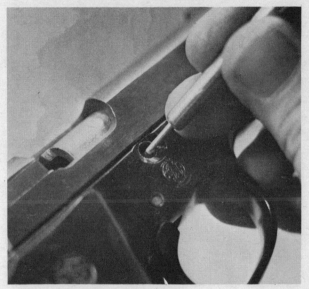

3. Remove the slide latch toward the left. Move the slide back to its normal position, and use the safety to drop the hammer to the fired position. Return the safety to off-safe, and move the slide assembly forward off the frame.

4. Grip the recoil spring and guide firmly to control the spring tension, and lift the spring assembly away from the barrel, removing it toward the rear. The slide latch plunger and spring, mounted inside the rear of the recoil spring guide, are staked in and should not be disturbed.

5. Turn the muzzle bushing counter-clockwise (front view) until it stops, then remove it toward the front.

6. Move the barrel slightly forward, then tip it downward at the rear and remove it from the bottom of the slide.

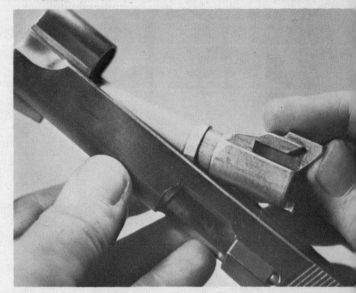

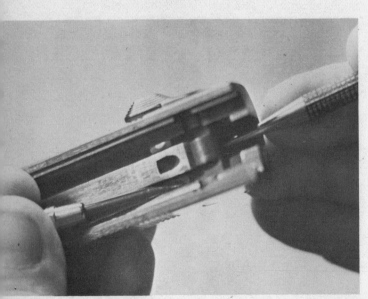

7. Depress the firing pin safety block, on the underside of the slide at the right, and use a slim tool to push the firing pin forward until it stops. Release the safety block, and the firing pin will be held forward.

8. In its forward position, the firing pin head will still protrude slightly into the safety cross-piece. Insert a tool to depress it to clear the safety, and push the safety, in off-safe position, toward the left. The small positioning plunger and spring at the lower rear of the safety cross-piece wil be released as the safety moves out of the slide, but will usually stay in their recess. Remove the safety toward the left.

9. Restrain the firing pin at the rear, and once again depress the firing pin safety block. The firing pin and its spring will be released for removal toward the rear.

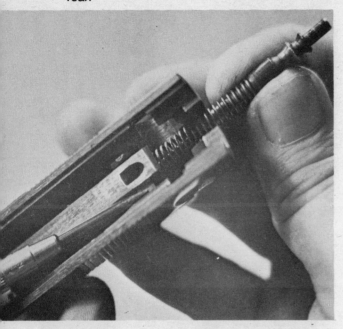

10. Alternately depress the rear sight hinge plungers on each side.

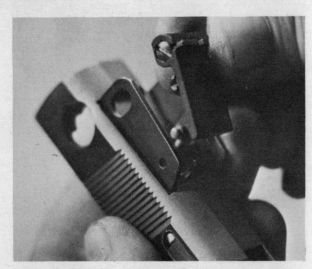

11. Restrain the plungers as they clear the sides of the sight mount, and remove the sight upward and toward the rear. Disassembly of the sight itself is not recommended.

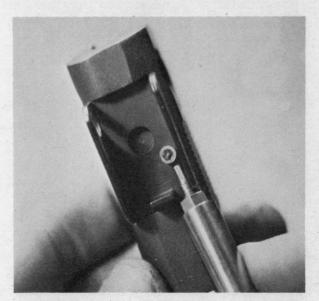

12. With an Allen wrench or screwdriver bit, remove the screw on the left, inside the rear sight mount.

13. Slide the rear sight mount out of its dove-tail in the slide, and restrain the two vertical coil springs that will be cleared.

14. Remove the firing pin safety block and its spring from the top of the slide.

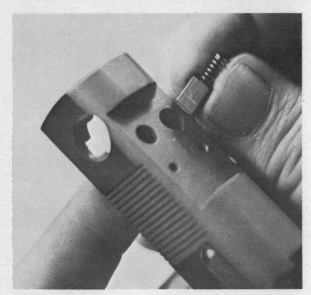

15. Remove the magazine safety plunger and spring from the top of the slide.

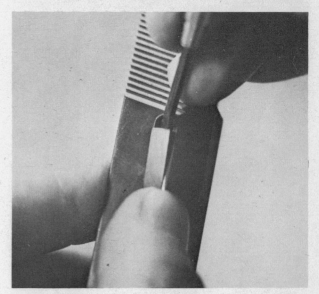

16. Insert a small sharp screwdriver between the extractor and its plunger, and turn the blade slightly, forcing the plunger toward the rear, and lever the extractor out of its recess. Keep the plunger under control, and ease the spring and plunger out toward the front.

17. With the hammer in the fired position, drift out the cross-pin at the lower rear of the grip frame.

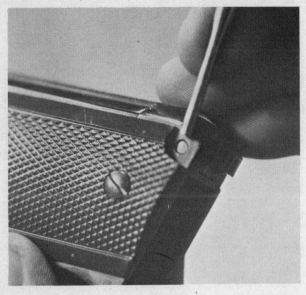

18. Push the lower end of the backstrap insert back until it clears its frame shelf, and it will be forced downward by the pressure of the hammer spring. Remove the insert downward and toward the rear.

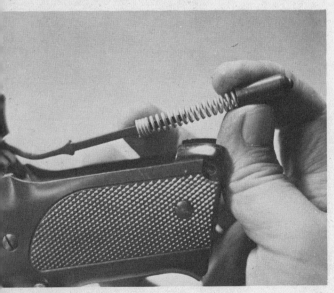

19. Remove the hammer spring plunger and the spring from the hammer strut.

20. Remove the grips. Push the hammer pivot about one-third of its length toward the right. Remove the ejector upward, and take out the ejector spring from its well in the frame.

21. Remove the hammer pivot toward the right, and take out the hammer upward. A roll cross-pin joins the strut to the hammer, and this can be removed to separate them, if necessary.

22. Move the sear trip lever slightly toward the left, then remove it upward.

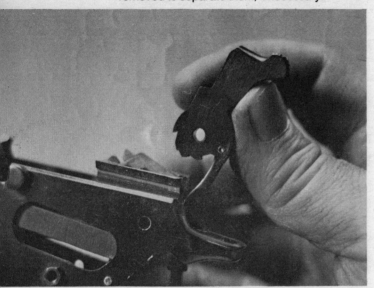

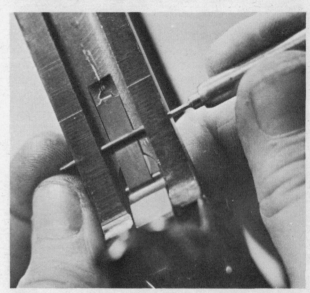

23. Move the firing pin block lever slightly to the left, then rearward, and take it out upward. Remove the spring that powers these two parts from its well in the frame.

24. Drift out the small cross-pin that retains the sear spring, inside the backstrap. This must be drifted out toward the right. Remove the spring toward the rear.

25. Push out the sear cross-pin toward either side, and remove the sear downward.

26. Turn the disconnector very slightly toward the right, to clear the trigger bar, and remove the disconnector downward.

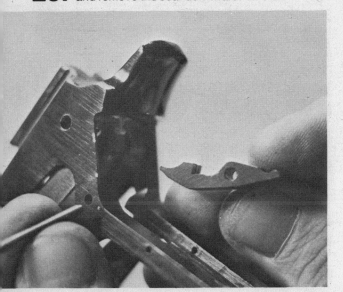

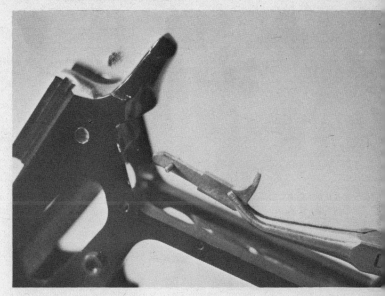

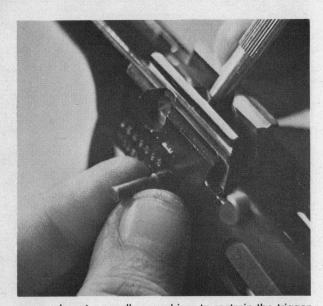

27. Insert a small screwdriver to restrain the trigger spring plunger, and push the trigger pivot pin out toward either side.

28. Allow the trigger to move downward, slowly release the tension of the trigger spring and plunger, and remove the trigger bar toward the rear. The trigger play spring, riveted in place on top of the trigger bar, should not be disturbed.

29. Remove the trigger plunger and spring toward the rear. Move the trigger to the rear of the guard, tilt it forward, and take it out upward. The trigger pivot retaining plunger and spring are mounted inside the trigger, and are retained by a small cross-pin. In normal takedown, these parts are best left in place.

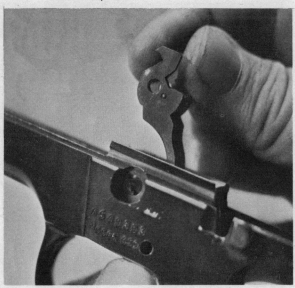

30. Depress the magazine release retainer, and unscrew the release button from the magazine catch cross-piece (counter-clockwise, left side view). There is a tool slot in the button, but in most cases the button can be unscrewed with the fingers. The button, retainer, and spring are taken off toward the left, and the catch piece toward the right.

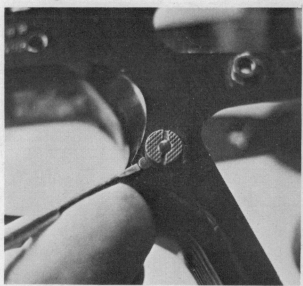

Reassembly Tips:

When replacing the sear cross-pin, note that the reduced tip must go on the right, to mate with the hole in the hammer pivot plate.

When moving the rear sight mount into place, alternately depress the two springs to avoid deformation.

1. When replacing the slide assembly on the frame, the ejector and the two small levers on the right must be depressed to go under the slide.

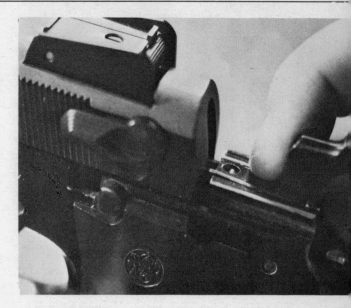

SECTION II

Many officers, especially those on duty in high-crime areas, have in recent years elected to carry a second gun, often known as a "back-up" piece. This smaller gun is often an automatic pistol, as this type is more easily concealed. If the regular duty sidearm is lost or temporarily empty during a serious situation, the back-up gun can save an officer's life. These guns also double as off-duty pieces, in departments having requirements that officers be armed at all times. The calibers chosen run the full scale, from 45 Auto to 22 Long Rifle.

AMT
BACK-UP

Data:	AMT Back-Up
Origin:	United States
Manufacturer:	AMT, Inc. El Monte, California
Cartridge:	380 ACP
Magazine capacity:	5 rounds
Over-all length:	5 inches
Height:	4 inches
Barrel length:	2⁹⁄₁₆ inches
Weight:	17 ounces

The ''Back-Up'' is made entirely of stainless steel, and, as its name implies, it is intended as a ''back-up'' gun for the law officer, for use if his regular sidearm is disabled, empty or lost during a serious social encounter. The little Back-Up is also popular as a self-defense pistol for the private citizen. The excellent and mechanically simple design is the work of John Raymond Wilkinson.

Disassembly:

1. With the magazine removed and the hammer in the fired position, use a non-marring drift to drive out the breechblock cross-pin toward either side.

2. With a non-marring tool such as a nylon-tipped punch or a wooden dowel, nudge the breechblock upward, working through the magazine well.

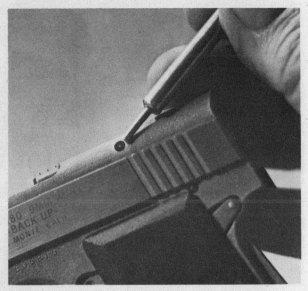

3. Remove the breechblock from the top of the slide.

4. Allow the slide to move forward until it clears the short slide rails at the rear of the frame, and lift the slide upward at the rear to clear the barrel. Move the slide assembly forward off the barrel and frame. Remove the recoil spring and its guide from the frame.

5. Drifting out the small cross-pin in the breechblock will free the extractor and its coil spring for removal upward. **Caution:** *Removal of the extractor will also release the firing pin and its spring, so control the firing pin as the extractor is removed.* The circular spring which retains the breechblock cross-pin is staked in place on the left side, and no attempt should be made to remove it.

6. Use an Allen wrench of the proper size to back out the grip screws. Lift the grip panels at the rear for removal.

7. With a small tool, detach the trigger bar spring from its groove in the rear lower edge of the trigger bar, and move it inward, behind the bar. Restrain the trigger, and remove the trigger bar toward the left.

8. Removal of the trigger bar will release the trigger and its spring to move forward, and it can then be removed toward either side. Take care that the small trigger spring is not lost.

9. Remove the safety lever toward the left. Take care not to exert outward pressure on the front of the lever.

10. Drift out the small pin at the top of the frame enough to partially release the ejector. It is not removed at this time.

11. With the hammer in the fired position, restrain it, and push out the hammer pivot toward the right.

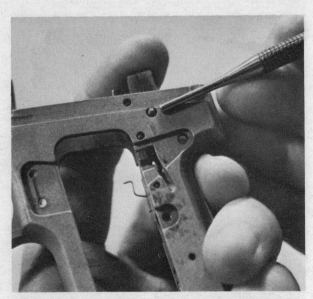

12. Ease the hammer out upward, along with its strut and spring, and remove the ejector, which will also be released. **Caution:** *The hammer spring is under tension.*

13. The hammer strut is easily removable from the hammer by turning it straight out to the rear and sliding it out of its seat in the hammer toward either side.

14. Drift out the sear cross-pin, and remove the sear forward, into the magazine well.

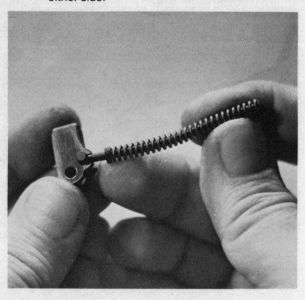

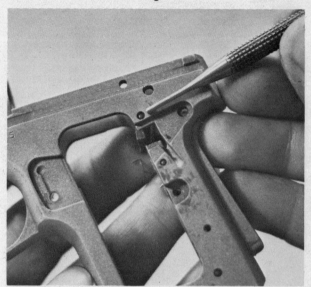

15. Push out the pin which retains the sear spring and the trigger bar spring. Before removal, note the position of the two springs to aid in reassembly.

16. Drift out the cross-pin at the lower rear of the grip frame, and remove the magazine catch downward.

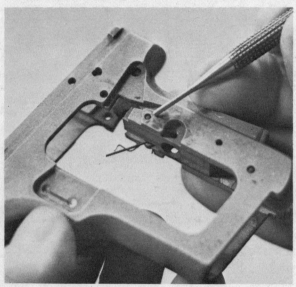

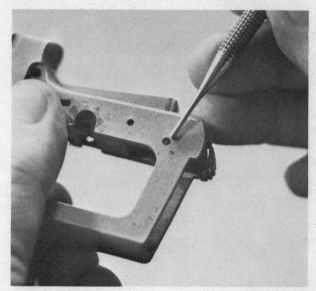

Reassembly Tips:

17. Move the grip safety upward to clear its lower lugs from the frame, then remove it downward and toward the rear.

1. When replacing the hammer and hammer spring assembly, be sure the spring and strut are attached to the hammer with the double curve of the strut in the orientation shown. When the hammer is in position, start the hammer pin through, then insert the ejector before pushing the hammer pin into place. As the hammer is inserted, be sure the lower tip of the spring strut enters the hole in the top of the magazine catch.

18. The inner tips of the grip safety spring are locked into holes on each side within the backstrap. Squeeze the inner arms of the spring together to clear the tips from the holes, and remove the spring toward the rear.

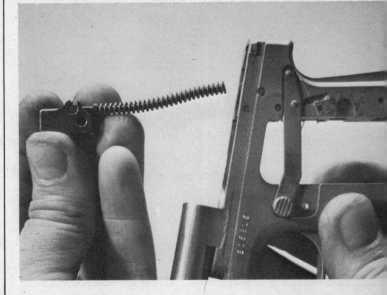

2. After the trigger bar/disconnector is back in place, insert a small tool to re-engage the trigger bar spring with its groove in the rear lower edge of the bar.

3. Note that the breechblock pin has a groove near one end. This groove must go on the left side of the gun, to engage the spring clip in the breechblock.

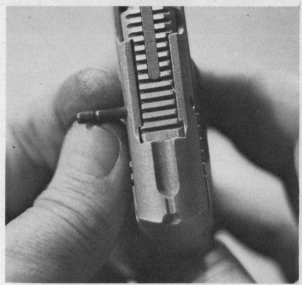

BROWNING BDA 380

Data:	Browning BDA 380
Origin:	Italy
Manufacturer:	Armi Beretta S. p. A. Gardone (Brescia) for Browning Arms Co. Morgan, Utah
Cartridge:	380 ACP
Magazine capacity:	13 rounds
Over-all length:	6¾ inches
Height:	4¾ inches
Barrel length:	3¹³/₁₆ inches
Weight:	23 ounces

Made for Browning by Beretta of Italy, the BDA 380 is essentially a restyled version of the Beretta Model 84, but the changes are extensive enough to give it mechanical features that are entirely different. This is particularly true of the safety and firing pin system, as the BDA has a slide-mounted safety with ambidextrous levers. A hammer-drop system is included in this system, and this also changes the frame components.

Disassembly:

1. Remove the magazine, and depress and hold the takedown latch lock button, located on the left side of the frame.

2. Turn the takedown latch lever on the right side of the frame down to the vertical position.

3. Move the slide and barrel assembly forward off the frame.

4. Controlling the tension of the recoil spring, lift the rear of the spring guide away from the barrel, and remove the spring and guide toward the rear.

5. Move the barrel slightly forward, then remove it downward and toward the rear.

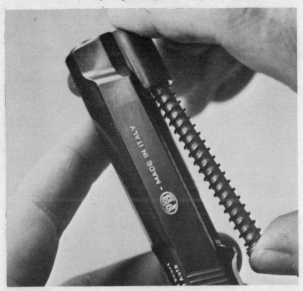

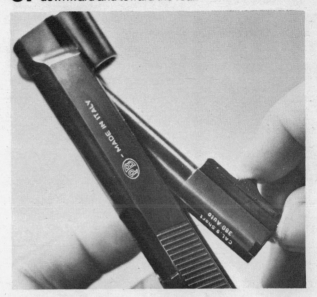

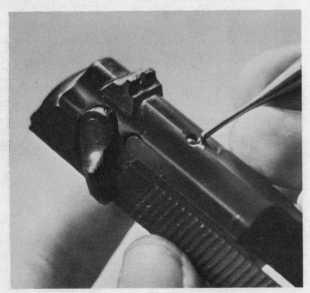

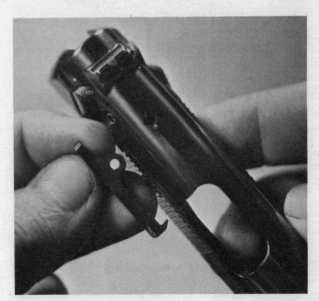

6. The extractor pin is drifted out upward.

7. With the safety in the on-safe position, remove the extractor toward the right.

8. Remove the extractor spring from its recess in the slide.

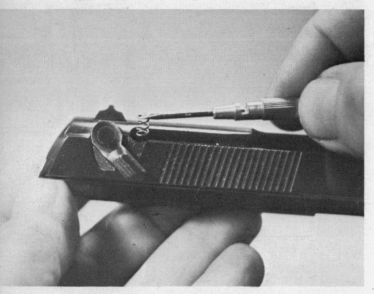

9. Use a small roll pin punch to drift out the roll pin in the base of the right safety lever, downward.

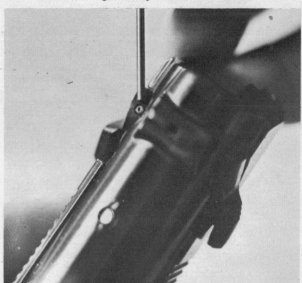

10. Turn the safety lever upward to clear its lower tab, and remove it toward the right.

11. Move the safety toward the left until it stops, and remove the firing pin from the rear of the slide. The safety must be in the off-safe position.

12. Be sure the firing pin spring is at the front of its tunnel, and remove the safety toward the left. The safety positioning ball and spring are staked in place, and should not be removed.

13. Remove the firing pin spring from the slide.

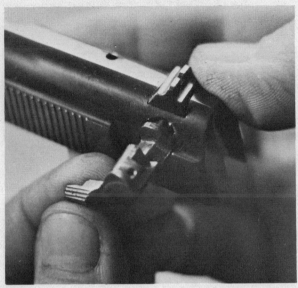

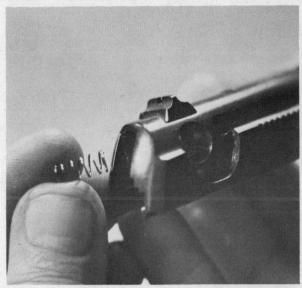

14. Depress the takedown latch lock button, turn the lever up to vertical position, and remove the latch toward the right.

15. Remove the grips, using a screwdriver with a wide and very thin blade. If necessary, grind or file one to fit.

16. Using the same screwdriver, remove the upper grip screw escutcheon on the right side.

17. With a tool or fingertip, unhook the lower arm of the magazine safety spring from its notch in the frame.

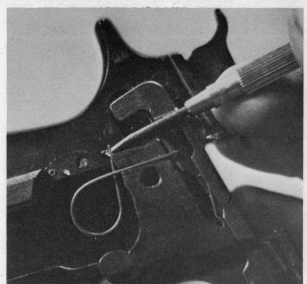

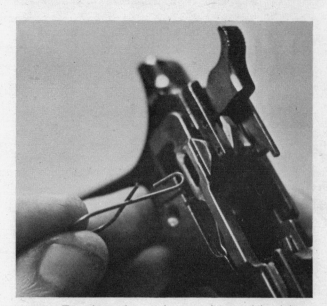

18. Lift the spring out of its slot in the frame, and move it inward to clear its upper loop from the opening in the trigger bar.

19. Turn the spring, and remove it toward the right.

20. Flex the upper arm of the trigger bar spring downward and outward, disengaging it from its slot in the underside of the trigger bar. Pull the trigger to give clearance, and lift the spring out of its recess.

21. Remove the trigger bar toward the right.

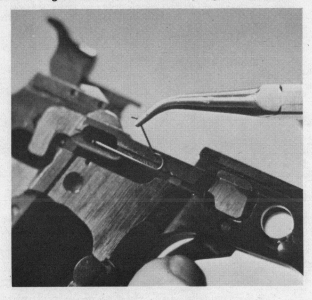

22. The cross-shaft of the slide latch is also the trigger pivot. Lift the slide latch at the rear to clear the frame, and move it slightly toward the left. Insert a small screwdriver to disengage the upper arm of the slide latch spring from its shelf in the frame.

23. Remove the slide latch toward the left, and take off its spring.

24. Remove the trigger spring upward.

25. Tip the top of the trigger down into the rear of the guard, and remove it toward either side.

26. Remove the takedown latch lock button toward the right.

27. Insert a tool to push the longer left block in the rear of the magazine catch toward the right, while pushing the catch toward the left, into the magazine well.

28. When the right end of the catch clears the frame, swing it inward toward the rear, and remove the catch from the frame. For left-handed shooters, the catch can be installed in reverse.

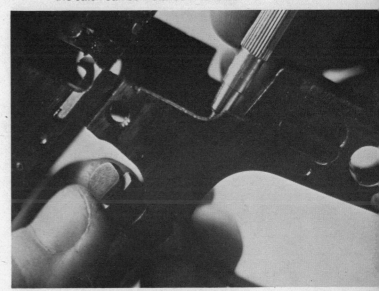

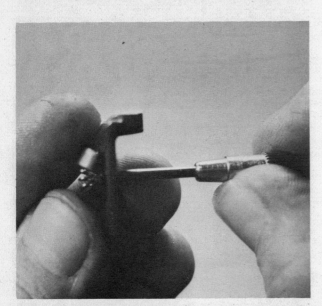

29. The retaining blocks and magazine catch spring can be removed, if necessary, by tipping the blocks outward. Control the spring during removal.

30. With the hammer in fired position, drift out the large roll cross-pin at the lower rear of the grip frame.

31. The hammer spring base should be forced out when the pin is removed. If it is tight, cocking the hammer will exert pressure to force it out. Remove the base plug from the bottom of the grip frame.

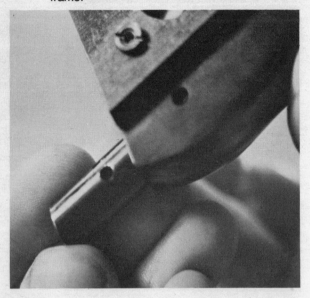

32. Remove the hammer spring and hammer strut from the bottom of the grip frame.

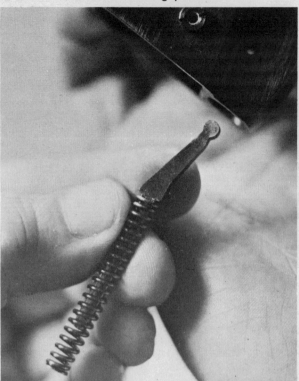

33. Push out the hammer pivot toward the left. Remove the hammer, upward and toward the rear.

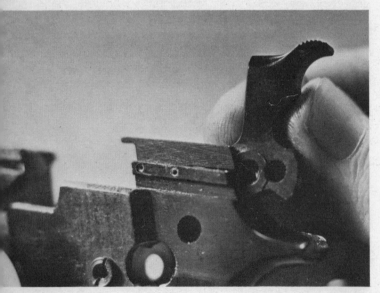

34. Restrain the hammer block to avoid loss of its plunger, and drift out the small roll pin at the top of the frame, just behind the magazine well.

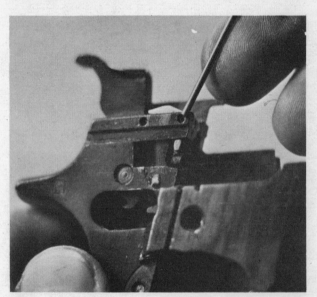

35. Keeping the hammer block under control, remove the safety sear trip (hammer drop lever) toward the front and upward.

36. Keep a fingertip over the rear to arrest the plunger, and move the hammer block toward the left. Ease out the plunger and spring, and remove them upward.

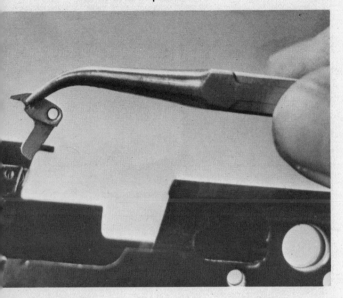

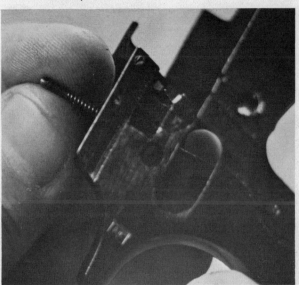

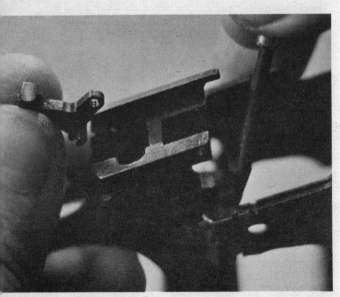

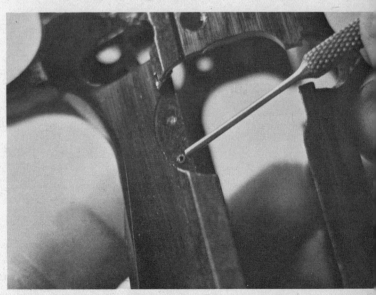

37. Insert a tool to tip the sear forward, and hold it there. Move the hammer block toward the left, then remove it toward the rear.

38. Drifting out the small roll pin below the sear pivot will release the lower tail of the sear sring, relieving its tension. Drifting out the sear pivot pin will release the sear and its spring for removal forward, into the magazine well.

Reassembly Tips:

39. Drifting out the other small roll pin at the top of the frame will free the ejector for removal upward.

1. The trigger, trigger spring, trigger bar, slide latch, and takedown latch release button are shown in the position they occupy in the frame. When installing the trigger bar, be sure the rear arm of the trigger spring is lifted to bear on the internal pivot of the bar. Also, be sure the forward tip of the spring enters its hole in the takedown latch release button.

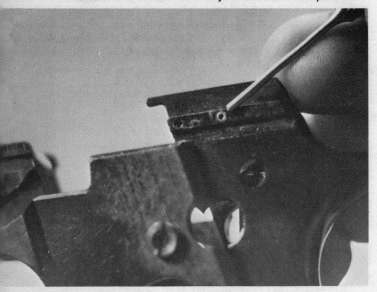

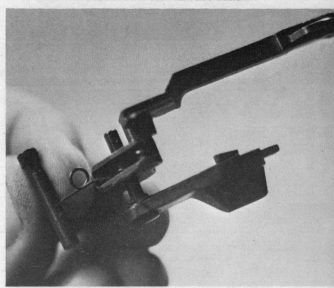

When replacing the hammer block in the frame, take particular care that the plunger and spring do not get away.

DETONICS MARK V

Data: Detonics Mark V
Origin: United States
Manufacturer: Detonics 45 Associates
Seattle, Washington
Cartridge: 45 ACP
**Magazine
capacity:** 6 rounds
Over-all length: 6¾ inches
Height: 4½ inches
Barrel length: 3½ inches
Weight: 29 ounces

The Detonics 45 ACP is the ultimate reduced-size, large-bore autoloader. The Detonics has features often found only on custom guns costing a great deal more. It also has several important innovations that are unavailable elsewhere. While the design is basically Browning/Colt, several important parts and takedown procedures are entirely different. All of the Detonics ''Marks'' designate options in sights, materials, and finishes, but the guns are mechanically the same.

Disassembly:

1. With the magazine removed and the hammer cocked, move the slide back until the semi-circular cut in its left lower edge is aligned with the rear tip of the slide latch. Push the tip of the slide latch cross-piece toward the left to start the latch out of the frame.

2. Restrain the slide assembly against the tension of the recoil spring, and remove the slide latch toward the left. Remove the slide assembly toward the front.

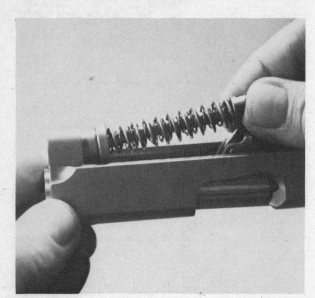

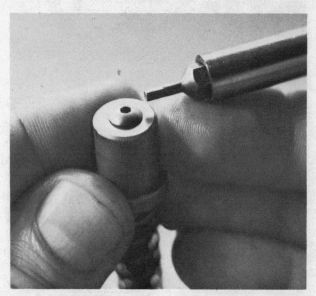

3. Lift the rear of the recoil spring assembly away from the barrel, and remove the assembly toward the rear.

4. If necessary, the recoil spring assembly can be taken apart. There is an Allen screw at the front of the forward sleeve, and removal of this will release the components to be taken off the guide toward the front. **Caution:** *The three recoil springs are under tension. Unless it is necessary for repair, the recoil spring unit should not be taken apart.*

5. Tip the barrel link over forward, and remove the barrel from the front of the slide. The link is cross-pinned to the underlug of the barrel, and is not removed in normal takedown. If removal is necessary, the pin is drifted out to the right.

6. Use a tool to depress the firing pin, and slide the firing pin retaining plate downward. **Caution:** *Control the firing pin and its spring as the plate is removed.*

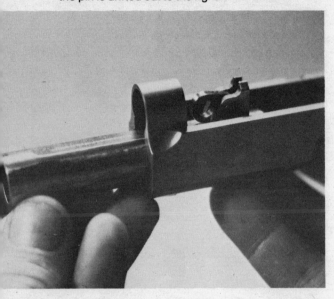

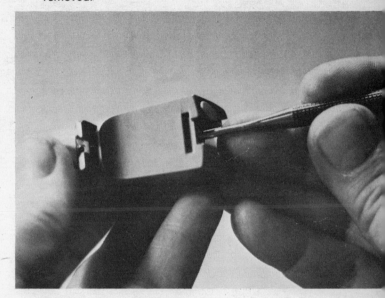

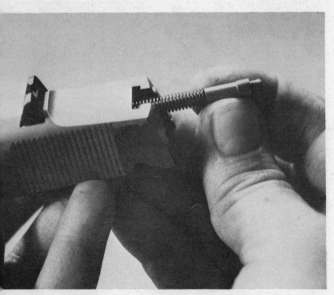

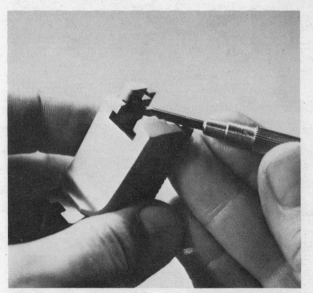

7. Remove the firing pin and its spring from the rear of the slide.

8. Insert a small screwdriver in the firing pin plate track, and lever the extractor toward the rear. After it is nudged out, the extractor can be grasped for removal toward the rear.

9. Backing out the vertical Allen screw at the center of the rear sight will allow the sight to be slid off toward the side.

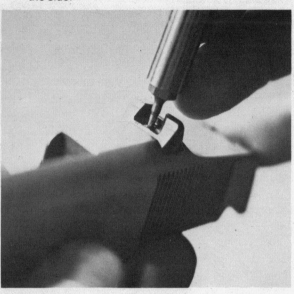

10. Remove the grips, and lower the hammer to the fired position. Drift out the cross-pin at the lower rear of the grip frame.

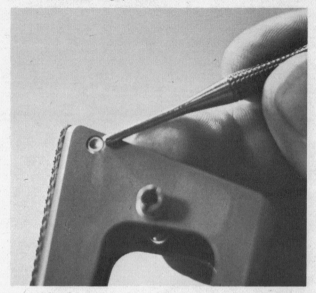

11. Slide the mainspring housing downward, and remove it.

12. The mainspring and its follower can be removed from the housing by pushing out the pin on the right side at the top, drifting it inward. **Caution:** *This is a strong spring, and it is under tension. Control it, and ease it out.*

13. Remove the combination sear, trigger and disconnector spring from the rear of the grip frame.

14. Move the hammer back to the cocked position. Turn the safety lever to its uppermost position, and remove the safety toward the left.

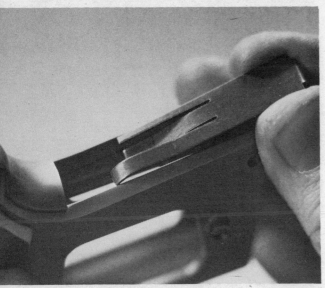

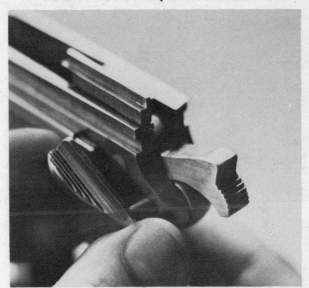

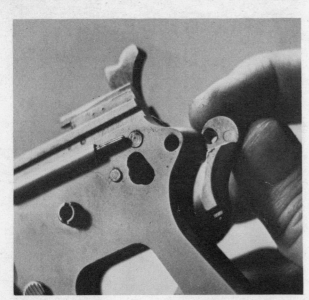

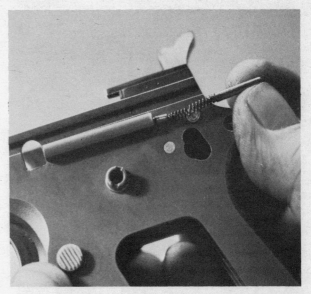

15. Remove the rear filler piece toward the rear.

16. Remove the safety and slide latch plungers and their common spring toward the rear.

17. Push out the hammer pin and remove it toward the left.

18. Remove the hammer from the rear of the frame. The hammer spring strut can be removed by drifting out its cross-pin, but this is not necessary in normal takedown.

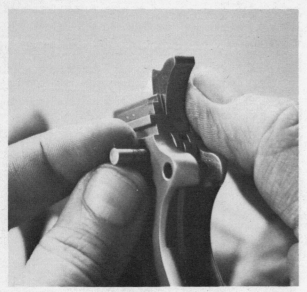

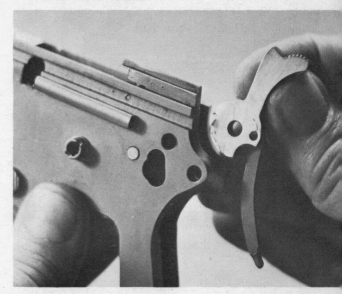

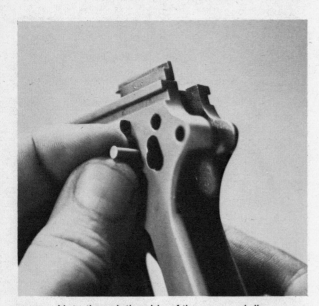

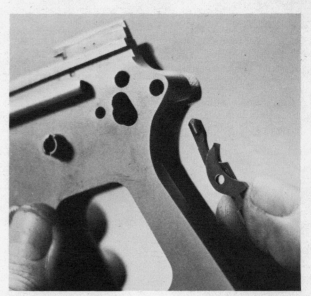

19. Note the relationship of the sear and disconnector inside the frame before removal. Push out the sear/disconnector pin toward the left.

20. Remove the sear and disconnector downward, then toward the rear.

21. Depress the magazine release until its button is level with the frame on the left side, and use a small screwdriver to turn the screw-slotted retainer on the right side counter-clockwise until it stops. Remove the magazine catch assembly toward the right.

22. Turning the retainer back to the right (clockwise) will release the retainer and spring for removal. **Caution:** *The spring is under tension.*

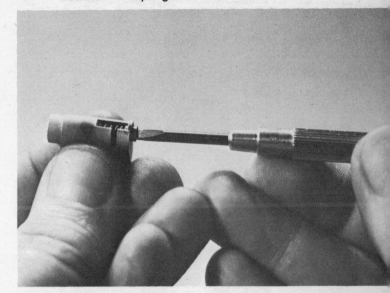

23. Remove the trigger toward the rear.

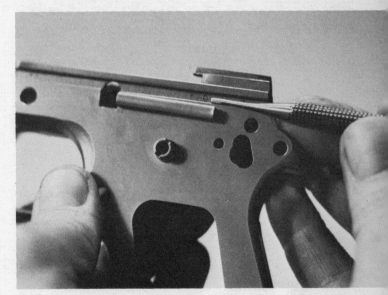

24. The ejector is retained by a cross-pin located in the slide track. The pin need not be drifted entirely out, just far enough to clear the ejector.

25. After the pin is drifted to the right, pry the ejector upward for removal, alternating the tool evenly to each end. The four grip screw escutcheons are also removable by simply unscrewing them, but they have very fine threads which are easily stripped, and in normal takedown are best left in place.

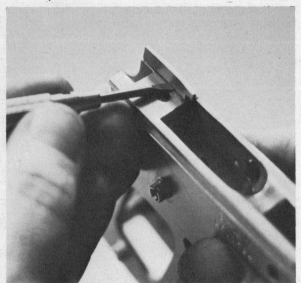

Reassembly Tips:

1. After the sear and disconnector are installed, put in the combination spring, hooking its lower tab into the slot inside the grip frame. Slide the mainspring housing partially into place, and it will hold the spring in position during the rest of reassembly. When installing the hammer, be sure the lower tip of the hammer strut engages the concave end of the mainspring follower.

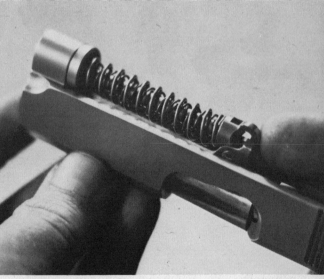

2. When replacing the recoil spring assembly, note that its rear endpiece must be oriented as shown.

FTL AUTO NINE

Data:	FTL Auto Nine
Origin:	United States
Manufacturer:	Wilkinson Arms Covina, California for FTL Marketing Corp. N. Hollywood, Calif.
Cartridge:	22 Long Rifle
Magazine capacity:	8 rounds
Over-all length:	4⅜ inches
Height:	3 inches
Barrel length:	2⅛ inches
Weight:	8¼ ounces

Very early examples of this neat little back-up piece have a small separate cover plate behind the top of the right grip, but except for this the mechanism is the same. This gun was designed by John Raymond Wilkinson, who also gave us the AMT Back-Up and the Terry carbine. Its tiny dimensions and large magazine capacity make it ideal as a second gun.

Disassembly:

1. With the magazine removed and the striker in fired position, push the slide rearward until the rear of the barrel is aligned with the exit cut for the barrel under-lugs, visible in the lower edge of the ejection port. Turn the barrel clockwise (front view) until it stops, bringing the lugs up into the port.

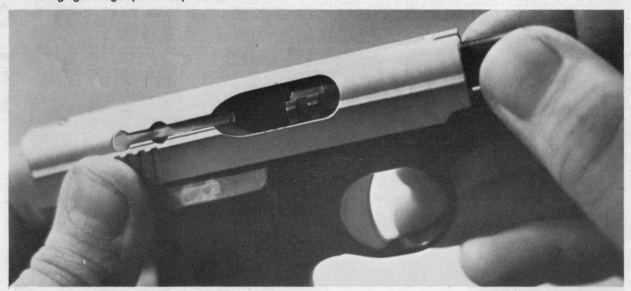

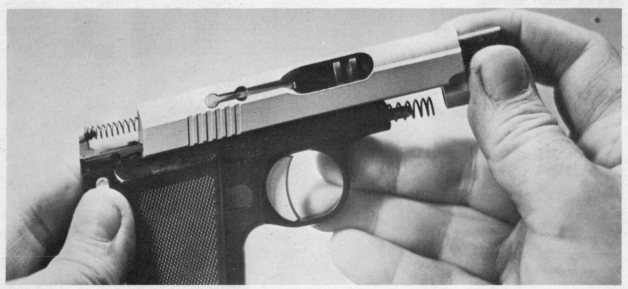

2. Move the slide and barrel assembly forward off the frame, and remove the recoil spring and its guide from the frame.

4. Rotate the barrel back to its original position and move it to the rear, against the breech face. The muzzle bushing can probably be turned with a fingernail, but if it's tight, an opened pair of sharp-nosed pliers can be used to start it. Unscrew the bushing, counter-clockwise (front view), and remove it.

3. Remove the striker from the rear of the slide.

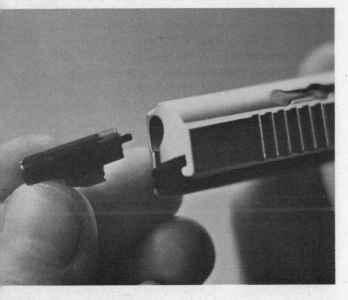

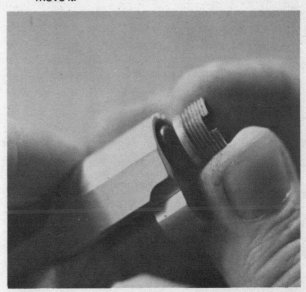

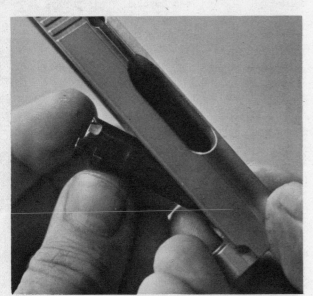

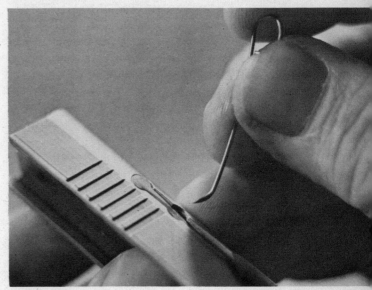

5. Move the barrel slightly forward to clear the extractor, then tip it downward at the rear and remove it from the bottom of the slide.

6. Removal of the extractor system is not easy, and requires one special tool. This can be made from a piece of steel spring-wire, the tip bent into a right-angle and sharpened. Diameter of the wire should be about .035″ to .040″. The tool is inserted in the middle opening of the extractor recess, and the sharp tip turned in between the two parts of the extractor. Be sure the tip of the tool is under only the outer extractor piece.

7. Use the tool as a lever to lift the rear end of the outer extractor piece from its recess, and move the outer piece toward the rear. Insert a card or heavy paper under the tail of the piece, to prevent marring of the slide.

8. When the outer extractor piece is started toward the rear, remove the tool, and slide the piece toward the rear until its side tabs align with the exit recess.

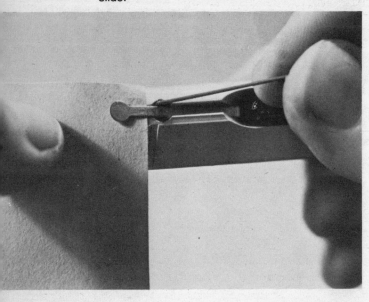

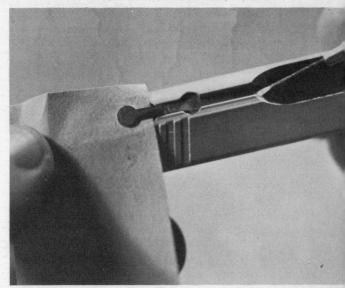

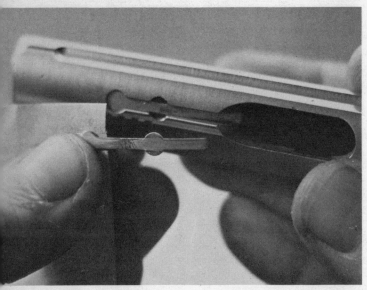

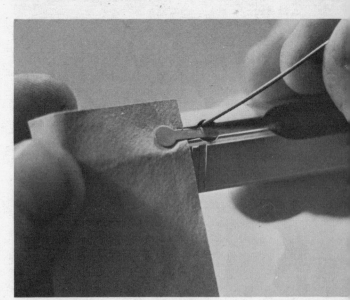

9. When the tabs are aligned, the outer piece can be lifted out.

10. Repeat the process with the extractor itself.

11. As the extractor is moved to the rear, it will be necessary to lift its beak at the front to clear the breech face. Lift it only enough for clearance, to avoid deforming it.

12. The striker spring will probably stay on its base post at the rear of the frame when the slide is removed. Pry it forward with a small screwdriver, and remove it from the post.

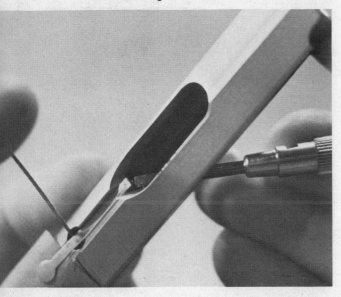

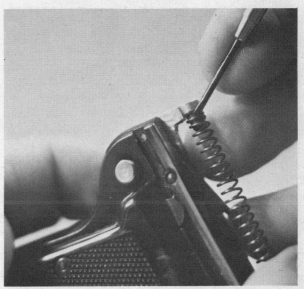

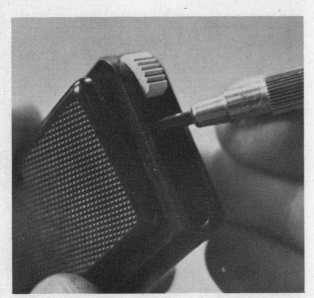

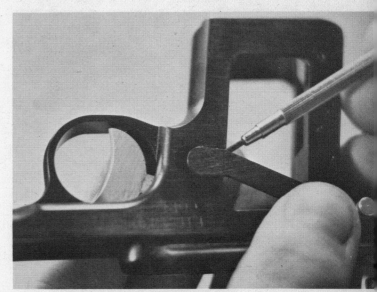

13. The grips are usually very tightly fitted. After removal of the grip screw, insert a tool inside the grips, and pry them gently outward at the rear, then remove them toward the rear.

14. Insert a small tool behind the trigger bar at the front, restrain the trigger, and lift the front of the bar slightly outward. The trigger and its spring will be released for removal toward the front.

15. Insert a small tool at the rear to restrain the disconnector plunger and spring, and hold a fingertip over the hole at the top of the frame to catch the plunger if the tool should slip. Remove the trigger bar toward the right.

16. Remove the plunger and spring upward. If the spring fails to come out with the plunger, use a bent paper clip to extract the spring.

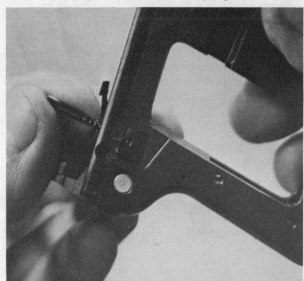

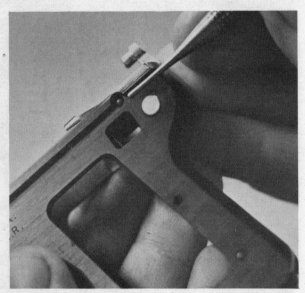

17. Restrain the ejector, and push the sear pin just far enough toward the right to clear it.

18. Remove the ejector upward.

19. Remove the ejector spring and plunger upward. Note that the plunger does not bear on the ejector, but is under the spring, to bridge the frame opening.

20. Restrain the sear, and push the sear pin out toward the right.

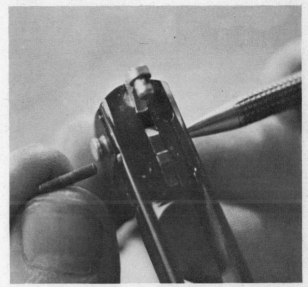

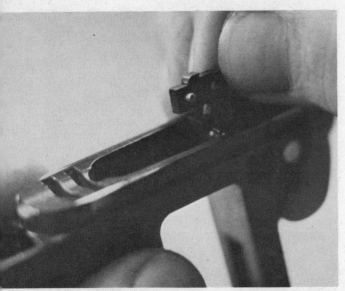

21. Keeping downward pressure on the sear, move it forward until it clears the frame, and slowly release the spring tension, taking the sear out upward. The small cross-pin in the sear is not tightly fitted, and can fall free, so take care that it isn't lost.

22. Remove the sear spring and plunger upward.

23. Use the extractor tool to lift the upper safety ball out of its recess in the frame.

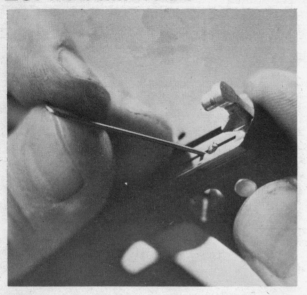

24. Push the safety to the left, to on-safe position. Grip the end of the safety with smooth-jawed pliers, and rotate it one-quarter turn counter-clockwise. Close the hole at the top of the frame and the safety tunnel on the right side with a fingertip and thumb, to avoid loss of the safety detent ball, as it will be released when the safety is taken out. Remove the safety toward the left. After the safety is removed, take out the detent ball and spring.

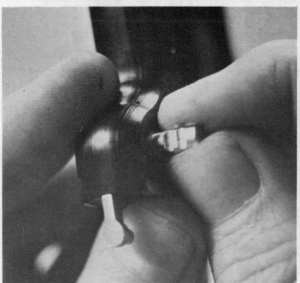

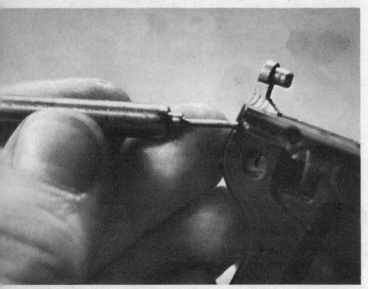

25. The striker spring base is retained by a cross-pin at the upper rear of the frame. Except for repair, it is best left in place.

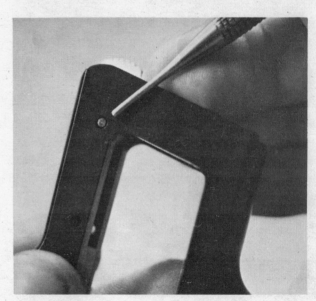

26. Restrain the magazine catch, and push out the catch cross-pin.

27. Move the magazine catch forward, then downward for removal. Remove the magazine catch spring.

28. Restrain the magazine floorplate, and remove the screw on the right side of the magazine. Slowly release the spring tension, and remove the magazine floorplate, spring, and follower downward.

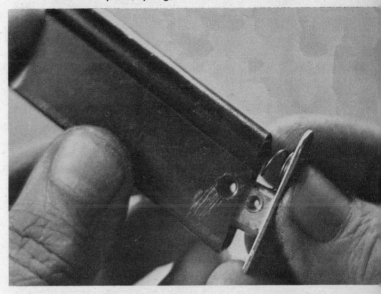

Reassembly Tips:

1. When replacing the safety system, be sure the two bevelled recesses are on the underside and on the left. Insert the safety from the right, and hold its left tip even with the ball and plunger hole while these parts are inserted. Use a tool to depress the ball, and push the safety across to the left while withdrawing the tool.

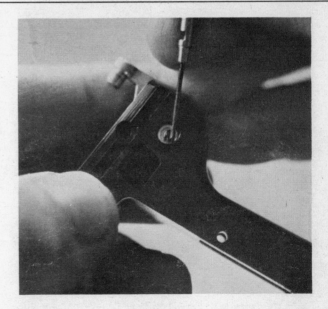

2. When replacing the trigger bar, insert a small screwdriver at the rear to depress the plunger and spring as the bar is moved into place.

3. When replacing the extractor, again use a card or paper to avoid marring the slide, and depress the extractor parts at the opening to align the tabs with their slots in the slide.

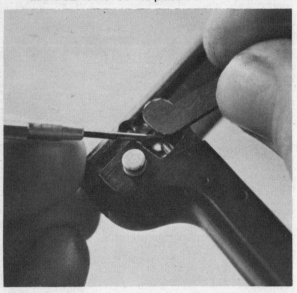

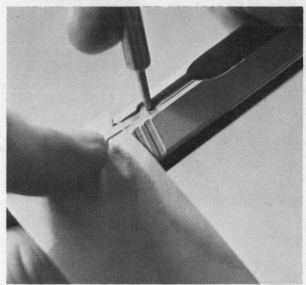

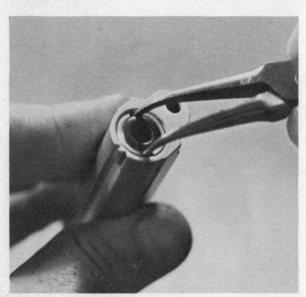

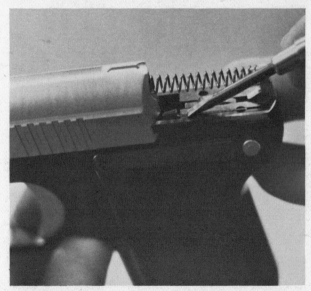

4. The barrel bushing will not loosen in normal use, but if you wish to snug it into place, a pair of sharp-nosed pliers can be used as a wrench, as shown.

5. When replacing the slide assembly on the frame, the ejector must be depressed at the rear to clear the slide.

HECKLER & KOCH P7

Data: Heckler & Koch P7
Origin: West Germany
Manufacturer: Heckler & Koch GmbH
Orberndorf/Neckar
Cartridge: 9mm Luger
Magazine capacity: 8 rounds
Over-all length: 6.54 inches
Height: 5 inches
Barrel length: 4.13 inches
Weight: 30.5 ounces

One of the smallest pistols made for the 9mm Luger round, the P7 was originally called the ''PSP,'' but received its numerical designation in the West German police trials. Notable for its gas-locked breech and squeeze-cocking operation, it is a fine choice for a back-up piece. Flat and concealable, it is never cocked until the squeeze-lever is fully depressed, and is instantly un-cocked when the lever is released.

Disassembly:

1. Remove the magazine, and depress the takedown button. Move the slide about one-half inch toward the rear, and lift the rear of the slide upward.

2. Remove the slide assembly toward the front. Remove the recoil spring from the barrel.

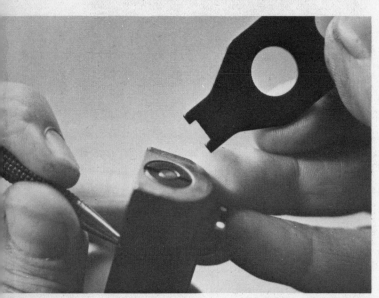

3. Removal of the firing pin assembly is easily done with the slide in place, before field-stripping, as the squeeze-cocking lever can be used to move the firing pin (striker). With the slide removed, it is necessary to insert a tool to engage the firing pin lug, moving the pin back until its head is even with the rear of the slide. Holding it in this position, use the tool supplied with the gun to engage the slots in the retainer.

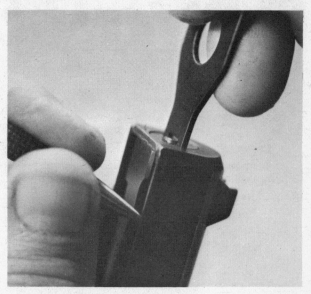

4. Depress the firing pin retainer and turn it 90 degrees to the right (clockwise, rear view).

5. Remove the firing pin assembly toward the rear.

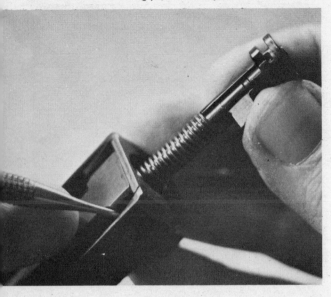

6. Grip the front spring collar and turn the firing pin lug out of its recess in the retainer, then remove the retainer toward the rear.

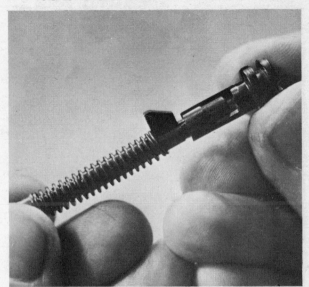

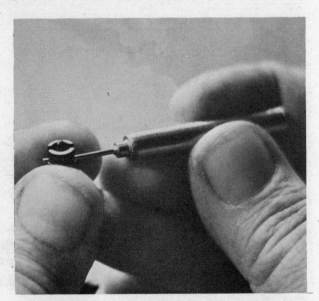

7. Restrain the spring collar, and push out the small cross-pin at the front of the firing pin. **Caution:** *The spring is under tension, so control it.* Take care that the tiny pin is not lost, and remove the collar and spring from the front of the firing pin.

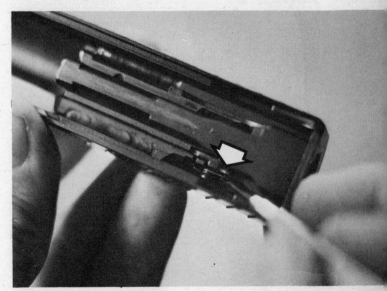

8. Insert a small screwdriver into the underside of the slide at the right rear, and trip the rear arm of the firing pin block spring from its shelf (arrow) toward the right.

9. Remove the firing pin block and its spring from the bottom of the slide. This is a captive spring, so there is no danger of loss.

10. Removal of the extractor requires a tool made of spring wire, about .040″ diameter. Insert the tool at the front of the extractor, in the groove provided, and compress the extractor plunger and spring toward the rear.

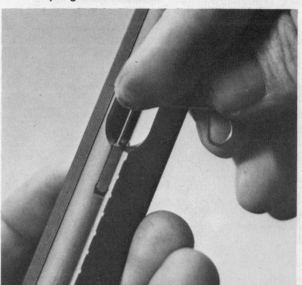

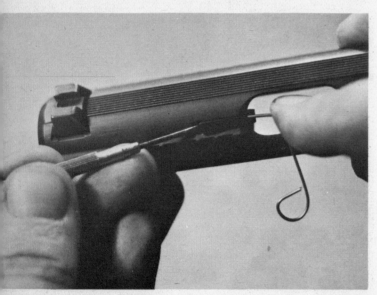

11. As the plunger is depressed, the rear of the extractor will move slightly outward. Keeping pressure on the plunger, use a small screwdriver at the rear to tip the extractor out of its recess. **Caution:** *The plunger and spring will be released as the extractor clears, so control them.*

12. Remove the extractor, and take out the plunger and spring.

13. Drift out the roll cross-pin at the lower front of the slide.

14. Remove the gas piston from the slide, and take out the compression spring mounted inside it at the front.

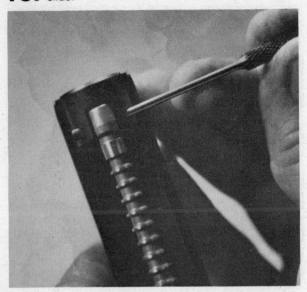

15. The reverse end of the firing pin tool is a screwdriver blade that fits the grip screws. After the screws are removed, lift each grip at the front, move it slightly forward, then lift it off.

16. At the upper rear or lower front, detach one arm of the cocking lever spring from its hook, and remove the spring.

17. Restrain the squeeze cocking piece, and push out the pivot pin at the lower front of the grip frame toward either side.

18. Remove the squeeze cocking piece toward the front.

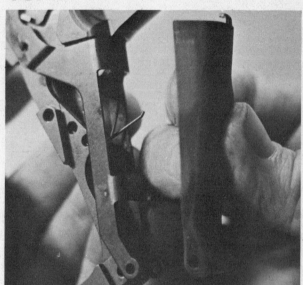

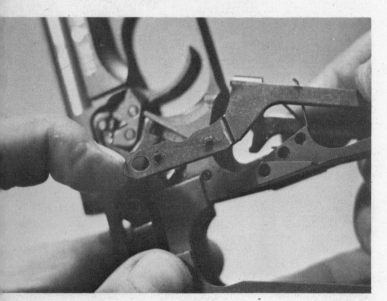

19. Move the lower arms of the drag lever forward until they clear the frame, then turn the drag lever toward the left side, and remove it downward and toward the left.

20. The cocking lever can now be removed from its recess on the right side.

21. If necessary, the spring which powers both the squeeze cocking piece and the drag lever can be removed by drifting out its roll cross-pin at the front of the grip frame.

22. Push the trigger cross-pin slightly toward the left, and the combination trigger and trigger bar spring will be released upward within its recess. Remove the spring upward and toward the right.

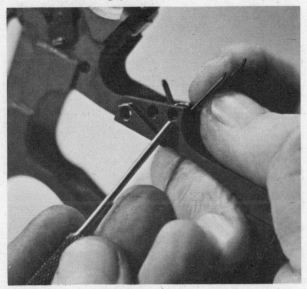

23. Push the trigger pin out, move the trigger forward, and turn it around toward the left for removal. The trigger bar is easily separated from the trigger.

24. Remove the disconnector toward the right.

25. Detach the rear arm of the ejector/slide latch spring from its shelf on the rocker, and allow it to swing forward, relieving its tension. **Caution:** *Keep fingertips clear of the spring as it is released.*

26. The two cross-pins having a wide flat head on the left are split and tempered on the right, locking them in place. Removal will require a shop-made tool of the same diameter, with a V-cut at its end to compress the end-leaves of the pin. Using a regular drift punch on these pins can break them. With the special tool, start the ejector/slide latch spring pin toward the left.

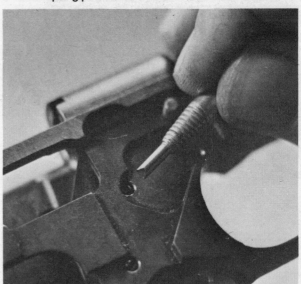

27. Move the ejector/slide latch off its post at the front, move it toward the rear, and remove it.

28. Drift the spring post out toward the left, and remove the spring.

29. Drift out the rocker pivot pin, again using the special tool. During removal of this pin, restrain the cocking latch, located on the underside at the rear of the trigger guard, as it will also be relased. Remove the rocker from its pin.

30. Remove the cocking latch and its spring downward.

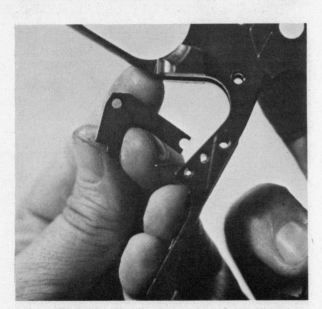

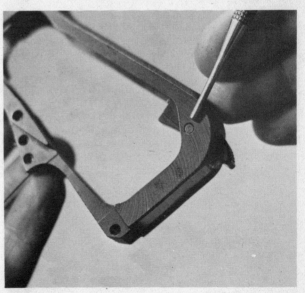

31. Tip the cocking lever stop over forward, and remove it toward the front. Note that the lower roll pin on which the stop rests retains no part, and need not be removed.

32. Push out the magazine catch cross-pin.

33. Remove the magazine catch and its spring downward.

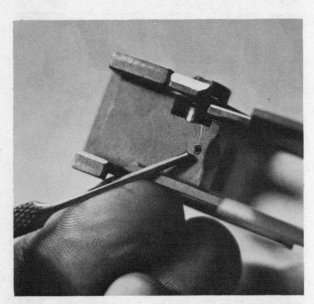

34. The takedown latch button and its spring are retained by a vertical roll pin at the top of the frame, and this pin is drifted out downward. The latch and its spring are removed toward the left. The cross-pin which pivots the ejector/slide latch and the disconnector also internally retains the barrel and gas cylinder. Removal of these parts is definitely not recommended.

Reassembly Tips:

1. When replacing the cocking latch and the lever stop, set the latch in place, taking care that its spring is seated in its well in the frame. Insert a drift through the hole to temporarily hold it in place. Engage the lower tip of the stop with the roll pin, and swing the stop over toward the rear, depressing the latch to clear its step. Insert the cross-pin, and withdraw the drift.

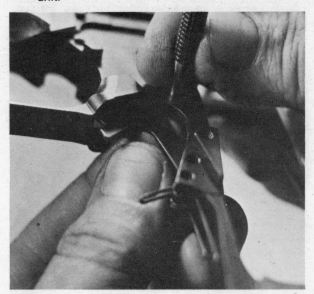

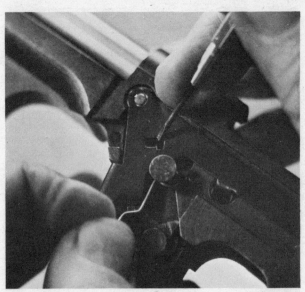

2. When replacing the ejector/slide latch, be sure the upper arm of the spring engages its hook on the inside of the latch.

3. When replacing the trigger system, set the trigger and attached trigger bar in place, and push the cross-pin toward the left until its end is even with the frame. Insert the spring, and use a tool to push it downward and toward the rear until it aligns with the pin, then push the pin into place.

4. When replacing the drag lever and the squeeze cocking piece, remember that the longer of the two spring arms powers the drag lever, and the shorter one powers the squeeze cocking piece. During replacement of these parts, the cocking latch must be depressed upward. The pivot pin is more easily inserted with the levers in squeezed position.

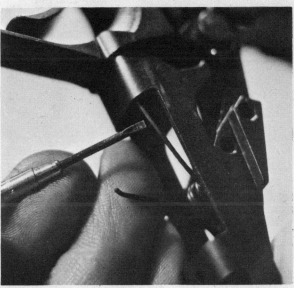

5. This photo shows the right side of the gun, with the parts in proper position.

6. This photo shows the left side of the gun, with the parts in proper position.

7. When replacing the piston, note that the cross-opening in its forward end is irregularly shaped. The piston must be installed as shown. During re-seating of the roll pin, insert a drift to prevent deformation of the compression spring.

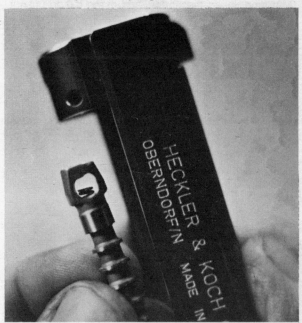

8. When replacing the extractor, use a nylon drift punch to push the extractor toward the rear, while restraining and guiding the extractor with the thumb.

When replacing the firing pin assembly, simply insert it into the rear of the slide, and turn the retainer until its slot is in vertical position.

SIG/SAUER P-225 (P6)

Data: SIG/Sauer P-225 (P6)
Origin: West Germany
Manufacturer: J.P. Sauer & Sohn GmbH Ekernforde
Cartridge: 9mm Luger
Magazine Capacity: 8 rounds
Over-all length: 7³/₃₂ inches
Height: 5¹/₈ inches
Barrel length: 3¹³/₁₆ inches
Weight: 28.7 ounces

The P-225 is essentially a shortened version of the Model P-220, the gun that was marketed at one time as the Browning BDA. However, there are several important differences, and all of the mechanical features are not exactly the same. For example, the magazine catch of the P-225 is a push-button type in a different location. One of several guns developed for West German Police use, the P-225 is also known as the P6.

Disassembly:

1. Lock the slide open and remove the magazine. Turn the takedown lever down to vertical position.

2. Restrain the slide against the recoil spring tension, trip the slide latch, and move the slide assembly forward off the frame.

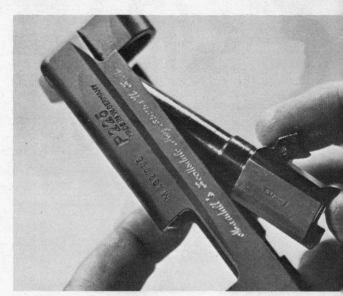

3. Lift the rear of the recoil spring guide away from the barrel, controlling the spring tension, and remove the spring and guide toward the rear. **Caution:** *This is a powerful spring. Don't let it get away.*

4. Move the barrel slightly forward, then remove it downward and toward the rear.

5. The breechblock is retained in the slide by a concentric double roll pin. Drifting out this pin will allow removal of the breechblock downward. The extractor is easily removed from the right side, and depressing the firing pin safety block upward will release the firing pin and its spring for removal toward the rear. When the firing pin is out, the safety block is released downward, along with its spring.

6. Turn the takedown lever until it points toward the front of the frame, and remove it toward the left.

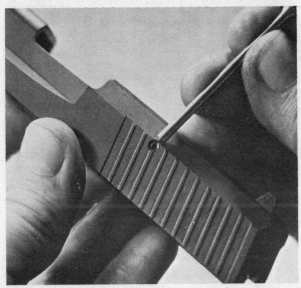

7. Removal of the takedown lever will release the locking insert. Move the insert upward and toward the front for removal. The attached slide latch spring will come out with the insert, and is easily detached toward the left.

8. Remove the grip screws. If the lock washers are loose, take care that they aren't lost. The right grip can simply be lifted off, but the left one must be lifted slightly at its lower edge, then moved off toward the rear, to clear the decocking lever.

9. Flex the rear tip of the combination trigger and trigger bar spring downward out of its slot in the trigger bar, and take the spring off toward the right.

10. Move the trigger pivot pin toward the right, just enough to clear the slide latch, and remove the slide latch upward.

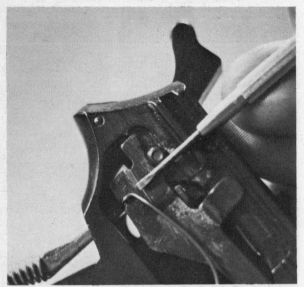

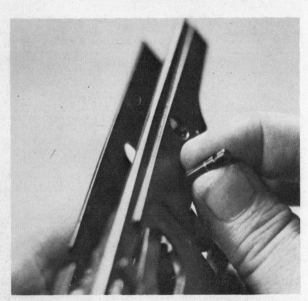

11. Remove the trigger pivot pin toward the right.

12. Move the trigger back against the rear interior of the guard, then move it forward and upward. At the same time, exert slight inward pressure on the trigger bar, until it moves into the magazine well. Do not use extreme pressure.

13. Remove the trigger and the attached trigger bar from the top of the frame. The bar is easily separated from the trigger.

14. Place the top of the frame (but not the hammer) against a firm surface, and use a screwdriver to exert pressure on the underside of the hammer spring base, lifting it out of its slots in the grip frame, and moving its lower end toward the rear.

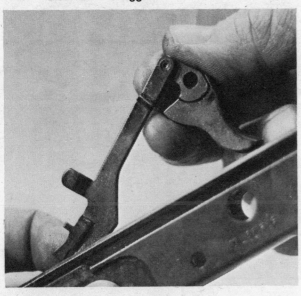

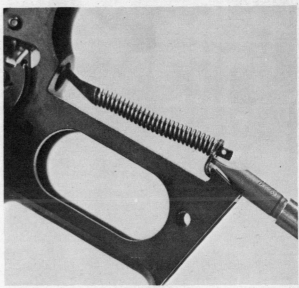

15. Remove the hammer spring assembly downward. The spring, hammer strut, and spring base can be separated by drifting out the retaining cross-pin, if necessary. **Caution:** *This is a strong spring, so take care and control it.*

16. Unhook the decocking lever spring at the rear, swing it forward, and remove it toward the left. The decocking lever post will be released at this point, and may drop inward, or may stay in place.

17. Remove the decocking lever toward the left.

18. Push the decocking lever post inward, and remove the post and its attached plate from inside the frame.

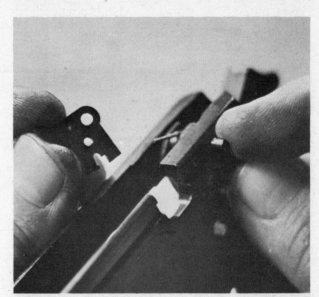

19. Depress the upper arm of the sear spring and move it toward the right until it clears its bearing pin, then ease it upward, relieving the spring tension.

20. Push the sear cross-pin toward the left, just far enough to clear the firing pin block lever. Move the lever forward, then take it out upward.

21. Remove the sear cross-pin, and take out the sear spring upward. Move the sear downward, then out the opening on the right side of the frame.

22. Push out the hammer pivot pin, and remove the hammer from the top of the frame.

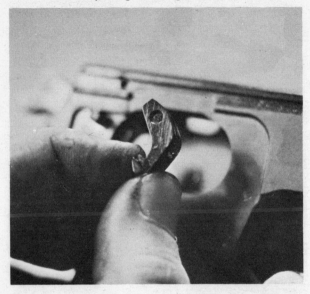

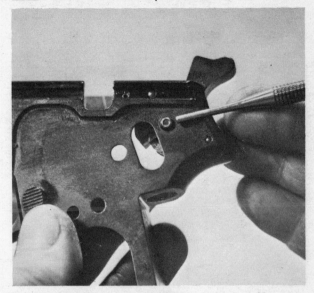

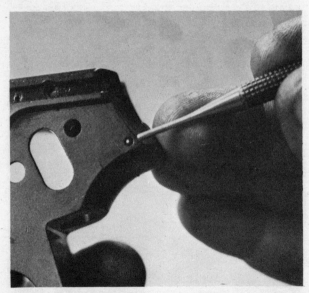

23. Drifting out the small cross-pin at the upper rear of the frame will allow removal of the hammer stop piece, and will also release the hammer rebound spring mounted in its center. *Note the position of the spring before the pin is removed, to aid reassembly, and restrain the spring during removal.*

24. Use a very small tool to depress the magazine catch retaining pin, located in the front face of the catch button next to the frame.

25. Remove the magazine catch assembly toward the left, and take care not to lose the magazine catch spring, retaining pin, and its spring.

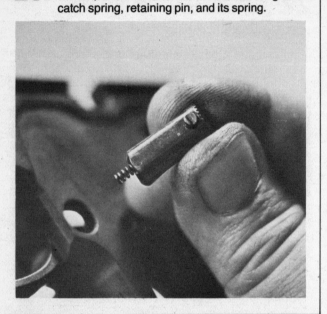

Reassembly Tips:

1. Note that there are two recesses in the trigger cross-pin, and these must be mated with the slanted slots in the locking insert.

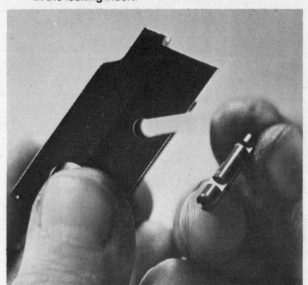

2. When the trigger cross-pin is installed in the frame, the two recesses must be oriented to the underside, angled slightly toward the front. A screw-slot is provided in the left end of the pin to aid adjustment. The locking insert should slip easily into place when the pin is properly positioned. No force is required.

3. Insert the takedown lever in vertical position, then turn it to point forward and push it into the frame. Remember to turn it back down into takedown position before replacing the slide assembly on the frame.

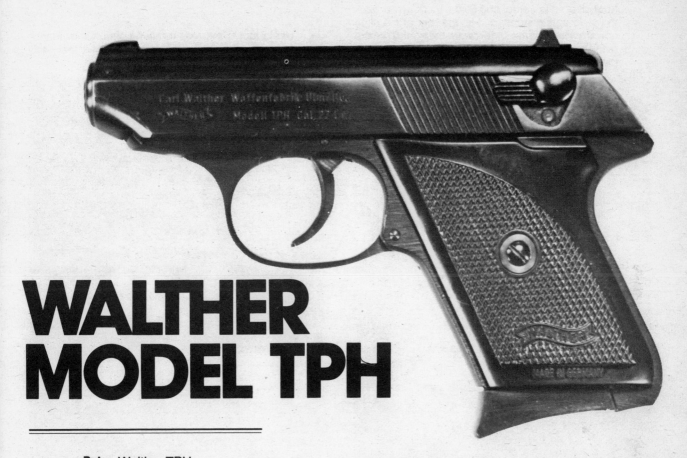

WALTHER MODEL TPH

Data:	Walther TPH
Origin:	West Germany
Manufacturer:	Carl Walther GmbH Ulm/Donau
Cartridge:	22 Long Rifle
Magazine capacity:	6 rounds
Over-all length:	5¼ inches
Height:	3½ inches
Barrel length:	2¾ inches
Weight:	11½ ounces

Until late 1980, federal regulations allowed individual police officers to purchase the elegant little Walther TPH from Interarms. Otherwise unimportable because of its size, the gun has not been available to the public. The regulations at this time, mid-1981, allow purchase only by law enforcement agencies. The TPH does not have the same internal mechanism as the larger Walther pistols, and the takedown differs accordingly.

Disassembly:

1. With the magazine removed and the hammer cocked, pull the trigger guard downward until its front clears the frame, and hold it there. Draw back the slide until it stops, and lift the rear of the slide upward. Remove the slide toward the front. Turn the recoil spring clockwise (front view), while pulling it forward off the barrel.

2. Use a tool to depress the firing pin until its head is forward of the safety cross-piece, and set the safety lever between its two positions.

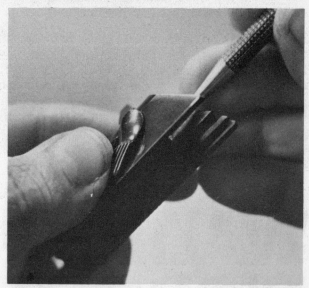

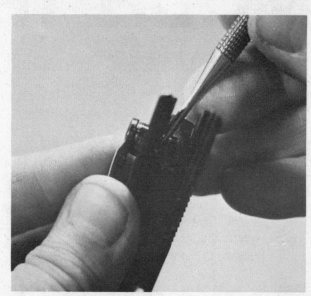

3. Use the tool to nudge the safety out toward the left. **Caution:** *The firing pin will be released as the safety clears, so control it.*

4. Remove the safety toward the left. Remove the firing pin and its spring toward the rear.

5. Removal of the safety will have relieved the tension of the combination safety and extractor spring, and the extractor can now be lifted out of its recess.

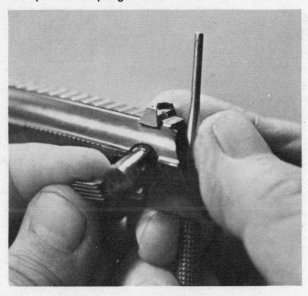

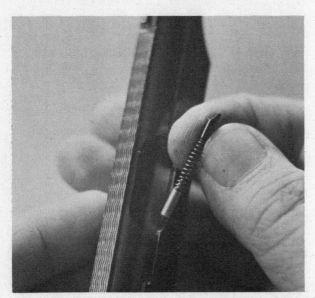

6. Use a tool at the rear to push the combination spring and its plungers forward, and remove these parts toward the front.

7. Remove the grips, and unhook the lower arm of the trigger bar spring from its stud on the frame. The spring is easily removed from its mounting stud, if necessary.

8. Pull the trigger slightly to the rear, and move the front of the trigger bar toward the right, disengaging its pivot from the trigger. Move the front of the bar downward while turning the top of the bar toward the frame, and remove it toward the right and downward.

9. Depress the rear of the trigger guard upward, and push out the guard hinge pin toward either side. **Caution:** *This is a strong spring, so control it.* Remove the guard, plunger, and spring downward.

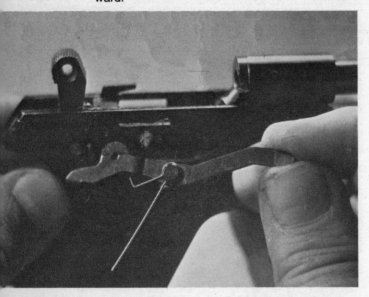

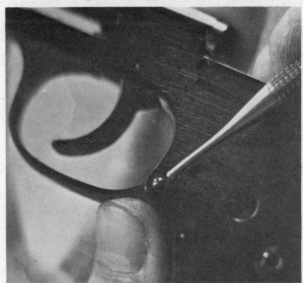

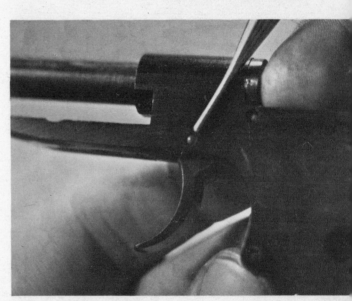

10. The small pin rearward of the guard pin retains twin levers which prevent movement of the guard when the magazine is in place. The levers are removed rearward, into the magazine well.

11. Drifting out the trigger cross-pin will release the trigger and its spring for removal downward.

12. With the hammer in the fired position, insert a small screwdriver inside the magazine well at the rear, and set its blade between the top of the magazine catch and the lower plunger of the hammer spring. Depress the plunger upward, and move the screwdriver toward the rear, pushing the magazine catch off its shelf.

13. The screwdriver will capture the plunger and spring, and the magazine catch will be released for removal downward. **Caution:** *Do not withdraw the screwdriver at this point.*

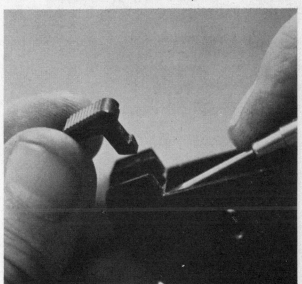

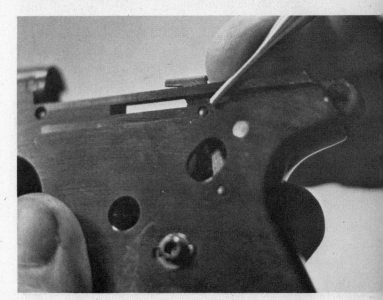

14. Hold a shop cloth over the end of the frame, or rest it squarely against the edge of the workbench, and withdraw the screwdriver. Remove the plunger and hammer spring downward.

15. Drifting out the small cross-pin at the top of the frame will release the ejector, insert block, and sear trip for removal upward. **Caution:** *When this pin is removed, the sear spring will be released into the magazine well, so insert a shop cloth into the magazine well to catch the spring.*

16. Drifting out the lower small pin will release the sear for removal forward, into the magazine well.

17. Drifting out the hammer cross-pin will allow removal of the hammer and hammer strut upward.

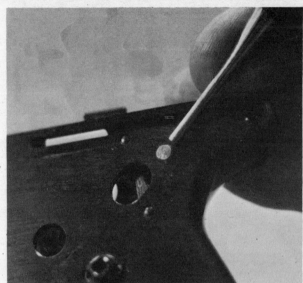

18. The barrel is cross-pinned to the frame. After removal of the pin, the barrel is pushed out toward the rear. In normal takedown, it should not be disturbed.

Reassembly Tips:

1. When replacing the hammer spring and its plunger, be sure the top of the spring encloses the lower shaft of the hammer strut. This engagement is visible through a hole on the right side of the frame. Insert a tapered drift punch (starting punch) into the hole in the plunger, and use it to push the plunger into the frame until it can be detained with a screwdriver blade while the magazine catch is installed. There is a slanted cut on one side of the plunger, and this must go toward the front.

2. When replacing the trigger guard assembly, insert a drift punch to hold it in place while installing the cross-pin.

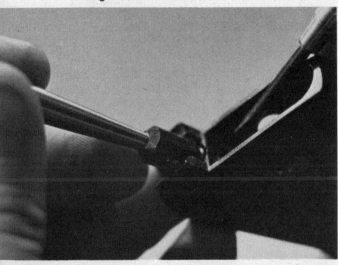

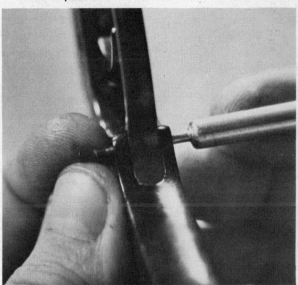

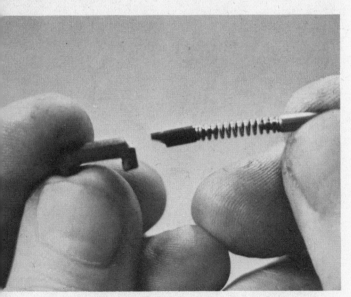

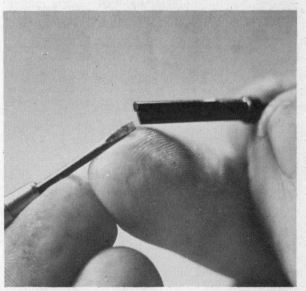

3. When replacing the extractor, note that the extractor plunger is shelved at the front, and be sure it is installed so it engages the extractor as shown.

4. When replacing the firing pin, note that its forward end has a narrowed, wedge-shape on one side, and this must be oriented downward.

5. When replacing the safety, insert a small screwdriver on the right side to compress the plunger toward the front as the safety is pushed into place.

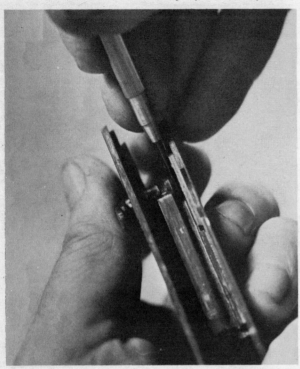

SECTION III

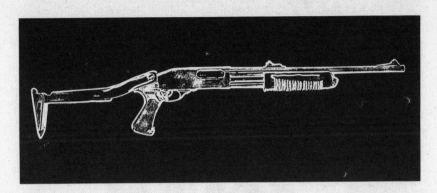

Essentially, today's police shotgun, or "riot gun," is simply a shortened version of a sporting shotgun, with or without an extended larger capacity magazine. In recent times, some additional accessories have become available, such as pistol-grip, folding buttstocks and shot diverter attachments. Departmental rules vary widely on the issuance of shotguns. While some reserve the shotgun for use only in riots or other special situations, others consider the shotgun a standard piece of equipment in the patrol car.

BENELLI 121 M1

Data: Benelli 121 M1
Origin: Italy
Manufacturer: Benelli Armi, S. p. A., Urbino
Gauge: 12
Magazine capacity: 7 rounds
Over-all length 39¾ inches
Barrel length: 19⅝ inches
Weight: 7 lbs., 3 oz.

The new Benelli semi-auto shotgun has an unusual action, using neither gas nor long recoil. Instead, it has a prop-type locking bar that is released by a rebounding bolt head—a unique system. Importation and sales in the U.S. are being handled by Heckler & Koch, Inc. There are also sporting versions of this gun, and the instructions generally apply to these as well.

Disassembly:

1. Loosen the cross-screw in the magazine tube hanger loop at the muzzle, and slide the hanger off toward the front. Cycle the action to cock the internal hammer, and set the safety in the on-safe position. Unscrew the knurled retaining nut at the front of the fore-end, and remove the nut and the sling loop toward the front. The nut unscrews counter-clockwise (front view).

2. Remove the barrel, upper receiver, and fore-end toward the front. If the gun is new and tight, it may be necessary to pull the bolt half-way back and release it several times, to start the assembly forward.

3. Tip the rear of the fore-end wood away from the barrel, and remove the fore-end downward and toward the rear. Remove the spacer ring and spring ring from the recess at the front of the fore-end. The rings will be released as the wood is taken off, so take care that they aren't lost.

4. Move the bolt all the way to the rear of the receiver, and pull out the firing pin retainer toward the right. A fingernail notch is provided in the head of the T-shaped retainer, and no tools are needed. Remove the firing pin and its return spring toward the rear.

5. Remove the cocking handle toward the right, and remove the bolt assembly toward the rear. The ejector, which is also the bolt guide, is welded in place inside the receiver, and is not removable.

6. Remove the locking bar from the underside of the bolt carrier, outward and toward the rear.

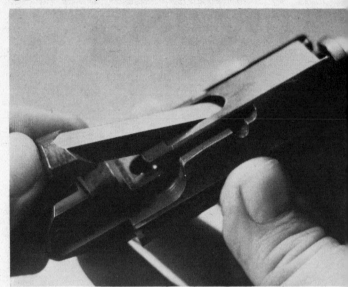

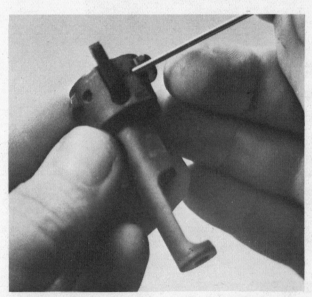

7. Remove the bolt head from the front of the bolt carrier. Remove the heavy bolt head spring toward the front.

8. The extractor and its coil spring are retained on the right side of the bolt head by a vertical roll pin. Restrain the extractor, and drift out the pin in either direction. Remove the extractor and spring toward the right.

9. The recoil spring connector strut is retained at the lower rear of the bolt carrier by a cross-pin that is riveted on both sides. Unless removal is necessary for repair, this pin should be left in place.

10. Drift out the roll pin at the lower rear of the lower receiver, directly above the safety. Push the carrier latch, and tip the carrier up to its raised position. Use a nylon-tipped drift punch to nudge the trigger group downward at the rear. Be sure the carrier stays elevated, or it will be damaged.

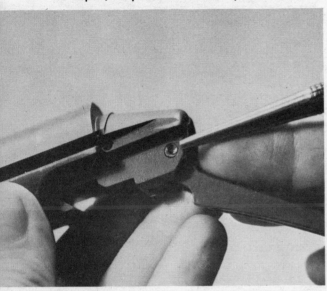

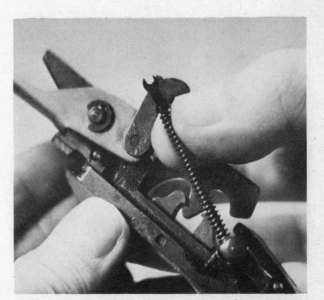

11. When the trigger group is free, remove it downward and toward the rear.

12. Grip the front of the carrier spring guide firmly, and move it toward the rear to detach it from its cross-pin in the carrier dog. Slowly release the spring tension, and remove the guide, spring, and spring base from the trigger group.

13. The carrier pivot is retained on both sides of the group by C-clips, but only one has to be taken off. Remove the C-clip from either side, restraining it as it is pried from its groove to prevent loss. Remove the carrier pivot from the trigger group.

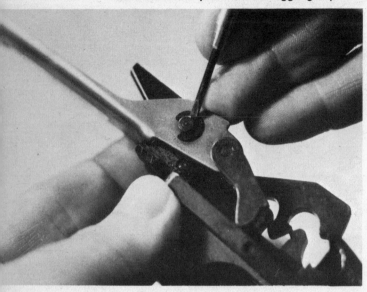

14. Remove the carrier upward.

15. The carrier dog pivot is easily removed, and the dog is then detached from the carrier. The pivot is held in place by the side of the group unit when the carrier is in place, and is freed as the carrier is taken off, so take care that it isn't lost.

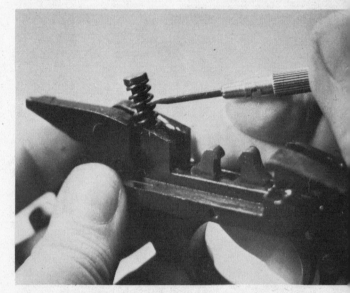

16. Move the safety to the off-safe position, pull the trigger, and ease the hammer over forward, beyond its normal fired position. The hammer spring and follower can now be removed upward.

17. Pull out the hammer pivot toward the right, and remove the hammer upward.

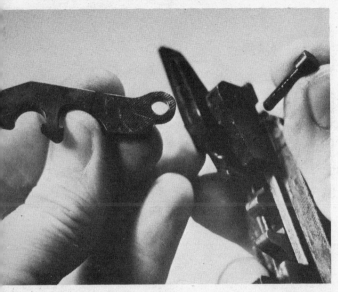

18. Restrain the trigger, and drift out the trigger pin toward the right.

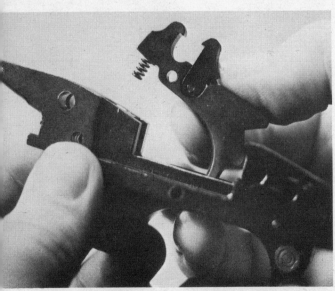

19. Remove the trigger assembly upward. The trigger spring is easily detached from the front of the trigger. The secondary sear, or disconnector, and its plunger and spring can be removed from the trigger by pushing out its cross-pin. **Caution:** *Control the plunger and spring as the pin is taken out.*

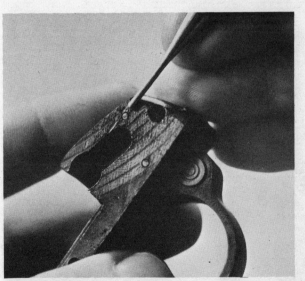

20. Hold a fingertip over the hole on top of the group at the rear to arrest the safety spring, and drift the small cross-pin at upper rear toward the right until the hole is cleared. Remove the safety spring and plunger upward, and push out the safety button toward either side. If the plunger fails to come out with the spring, tap the trigger group on the workbench to free it. The other small cross-pin at the rear of the group is a limit pin for the trigger. It retains no part, and need not be removed in normal takedown.

21. The carrier latch and its spring are retained inside the right wall of the lower receiver by a vertical pin which is pushed out upward. Only half of the lower tip of the pin is accessible, and a very small screwdriver or an opened paper clip should be used to push the pin. Restrain the carrier latch.

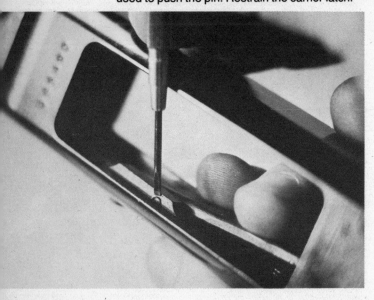

22. After the pin is pushed out, remove the carrier latch from the lower receiver. The spring is easily detached from the carrier latch, if necessary.

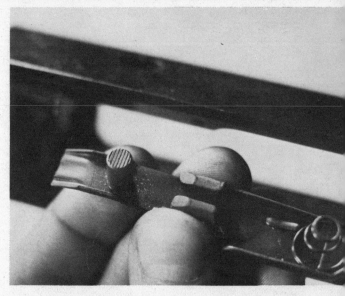

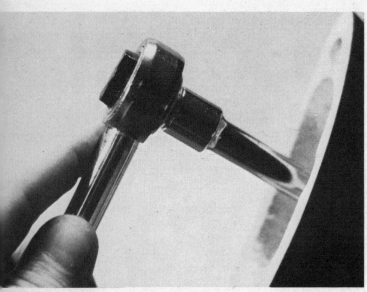

23. An ordinary socket wrench can be used to remove the nut under the buttplate that retains the stock. The exact size of the nut is 13mm, but if no metric socket is available, a standard ½-inch socket will work. Take off the nut, lock washer, and spacer washer, and remove the buttstock toward the rear.

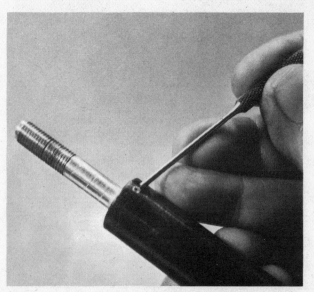

24. Drifting out the vertical roll pin at the rear of the recoil spring housing will release the stock mounting bolt for removal toward the rear. **Caution:** *The stock bolt is also the retainer for the recoil spring, so restrain it during removal.* Take out the spring and follower toward the rear. No attempt should be made to remove the spring housing or the magazine assembly from the lower receiver.

Reassembly Tips:

1. When replacing the safety button in the trigger group, remember that the end with the red band goes on the left side.

2. When replacing the carrier spring base in its recess on the left side of the trigger group, note that the hole in the base is off-center. The end nearest to the hole must go toward the outside—that is, to the left. Also, the flat face of the base goes to the front.

The bolt head must be pushed to its rear position in the carrier before the cocking handle can be re-inserted.

When replacing the two rings in the front of the fore-end, the plain ring goes in first, and the spring ring at the front.

When moving the barrel and receiver assembly toward the rear, be sure the rear tip of the recoil spring strut on the bolt carrier engages the cup of the spring follower.

ITHACA MODEL 37R

Data:	Ithaca Model 37R
Origin:	United States
Manufacturer:	Ithaca Gun Company Ithaca, New York
Gauge:	12
Magazine Capacity:	7 rounds
Over-all length:	39½ inches
Barrel length:	19½ inches
Weight:	7 pounds

In its full police mode, the Ithaca slide-action gun has an extended seven-shot magazine tube, a Parkerized finish, and sling swivels as standard equipment. Internally, its mechanism is the same as the sporting models of this gun, and the instructions can be applied to those as well.

Disassembly:

1. Operate the slide latch, and move the bolt to the rear. Turn the magazine endcap clockwise (front view) until it stops.

2. Turn the barrel counter-clockwise (front view) until it stops, and remove the barrel toward the front.

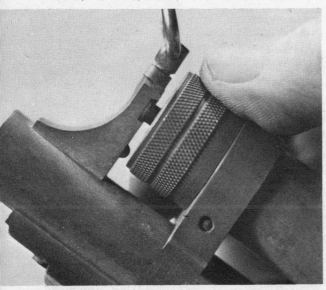

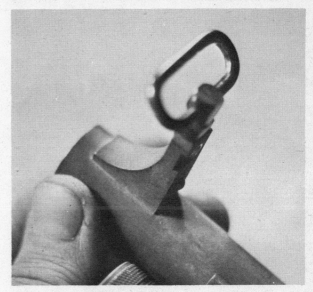

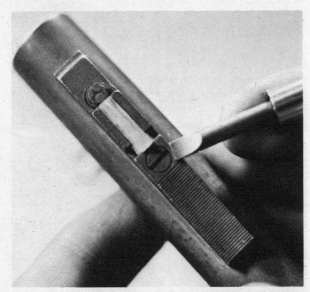

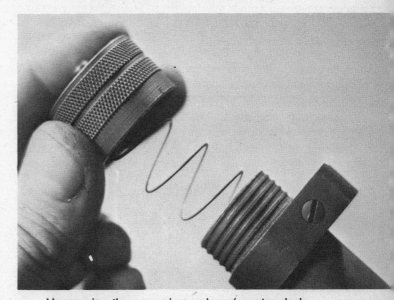

3. The front sight blade can be removed by depressing the plunger in front and sliding the blade forward. Removal of the large screw on top of the sight does not necessarily release the sight, as many sight bases are silver-soldered in place.

4. Unscrewing the magazine endcap (counter-clockwise, front view) will release the magazine spring and follower for removal toward the front. Control the magazine spring as the cap is removed. The cross-screw in the magazine yoke can now be taken out, and the yoke nudged off toward the front.

5. Insert a small screwdriver through the loading port to engage a groove in the action slide retaining plunger, and move the plunger toward the right, holding it there while the action slide assembly is taken off toward the front.

6. Use a steel plate or bar of suitable dimensions to engage the notches in the fore-end cap nut, and unscrew the nut counter-clockwise (front view). The fore-end tube and attached action bar can then be removed toward the rear.

7. Remove the buttplate, and use a B-Square stock tool or a long-shanked screwdriver to back out the stock bolt. Take off the buttstock toward the rear.

8. With the bolt forward in battery, pull the trigger to drop the hammer to the fired position. Remove the large cross-screw at the lower rear edge of the receiver.

9. Move the trigger group out to the rear, then remove it downward. Note that this can be done *only* with the hammer in the fired position.

10. The right shell stop can now be moved inward and taken out the bottom of the receiver.

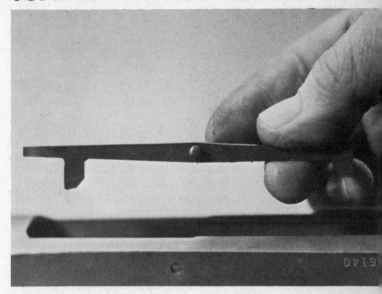

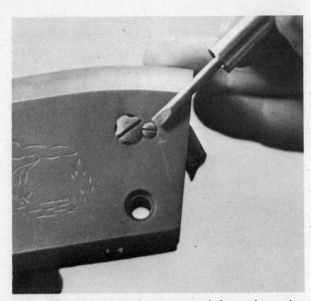

11. Remove the lock screws and the main carrier pivot screws on each side of the receiver.

12. Move the bolt to the rear, and remove the carrier from the rear of the receiver.

13. Remove the bolt and action slide piece from the rear of the receiver.

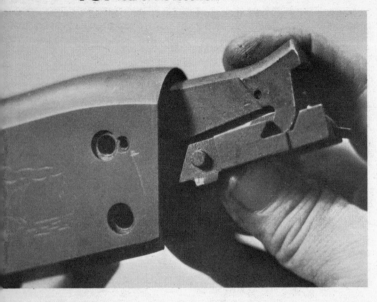

14. The left shell stop is retained in the left wall of the receiver by a small vertical screw in the lower edge of the receiver.

15. Move the left shell stop inward, then remove it from the bottom of the receiver, along with its spring.

16. With the hammer in the fired position, insert a tool at the rear of the trigger group to restrain the hammer spring button, and push out the retaining cross-pin. **Caution:** *Keep the button under control, as the hammer spring is powerful.*

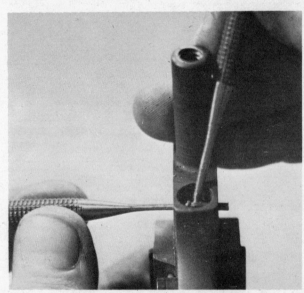

17. Remove the hammer spring button, the spring, and the plunger toward the rear.

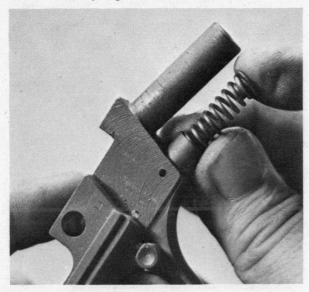

18. Drift out the hammer cross-pin toward the left.

19. Remove the hammer upward. If necessary, the hammer strut can be removed by drifting out its cross-pin.

20. Drift the trigger cross-pin about half-way out toward the left.

21. Remove the slide latch upward, along with its attached release spring. Remove the slide latch spring from its well in the trigger group.

22. The slide latch release spring can be removed by flexing it downward to clear the stud, and taking it off toward the right. In normal takedown, it is best left in place.

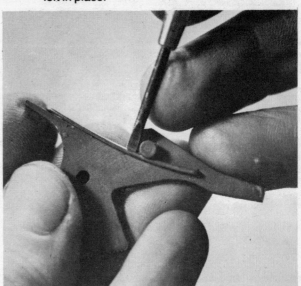

23. Push the trigger pin out toward the left, and remove the trigger upward. The trigger spring can now be removed from its well in the housing.

24. Push the safety out toward the right, and remove the safety plunger and spring downward.

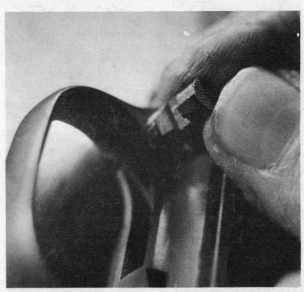

25. Detach the action slide piece from the bottom of the bolt. The slide bar retaining plunger is retained by a vertical pin which is driven out upward, and the plunger and spring can then be removed toward the left.

26. Drift out the cross-pin at the rear of the bolt, and remove the firing pin and its spring toward the rear.

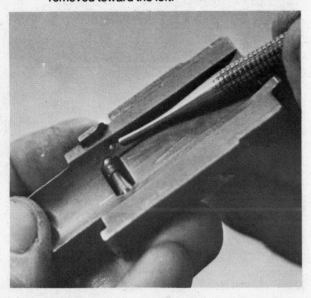

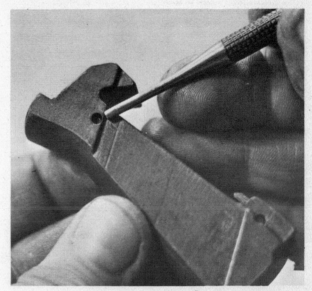

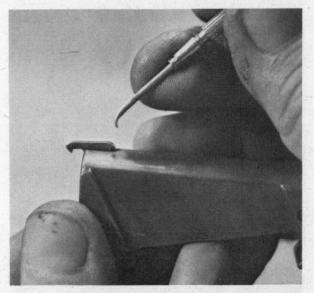

27. Drift out the cross-pin at the lower front of the bolt, and remove the lower extractor and its spring downward.

28. For removal of the upper extractor, a special tool is required. This can be made by heating and bending the tip of a small screwdriver, as shown. Insert the tool at the rear of the extractor to depress the plunger toward the rear, and lift the extractor out of its recess. Keep the plunger and spring under control, and ease them out for removal toward the front.

Reassembly Tips:

1. If the left shell stop has been installed prior to replacement of the bolt in the receiver, it will be necessary to depress the front of the shell stop to clear its rear upper projection for passage of the bolt and action slide piece.

2. When installing the carrier, move the bolt all the way to the rear, insert the carrier until it stops, then move the bolt and carrier together toward the front and align the carrier pivot holes.

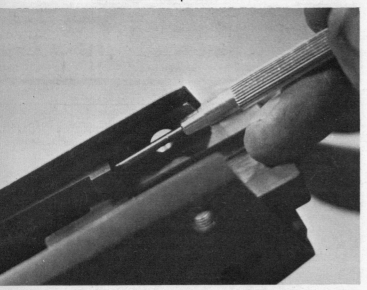

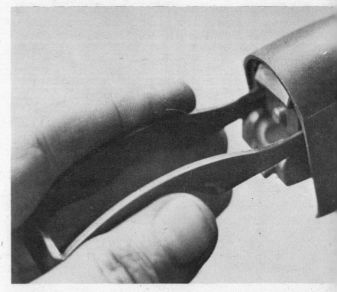

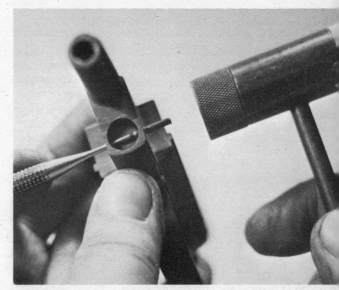

3. When replacing the hammer system, it will be necessary to lift the hammer strut to insure that its rear tip engages the cup at the front of the plunger, as shown.

4. When replacing the hammer spring system, depress the button and insert a drift punch to retain the button until the pin is replaced.

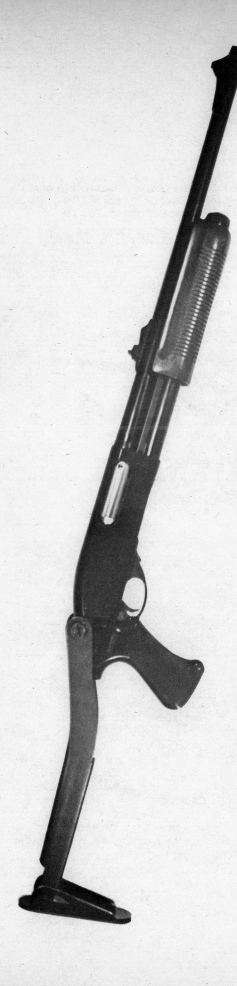

REMINGTON MODEL 870R

Data:	Remington Model 870R
Origin:	United States
Manufacturer:	Remington Arms Company Bridgeport, Connecticut
Gauge:	12
Magazine capacity:	4 rounds
Over-all length:	40⅜ inches (stock extended) 29⅞ inches (stock folded)
Barrel length:	20 inches
Weight:	8 pounds

In police use, the basic Remington 870 will often be found with the factory pistol-grip folding stock, and a short barrel equipped with rifle-type sights. Extended magazine tubes are also available, and sling swivels are often added. Except for the police accessories, the 870R is internally the same as the regular sporting 870, and the instructions can be applied to either gun.

Disassembly:

1. Open the action, and unscrew the magazine endcap. Take off the barrel toward the front.

2. Fold the collapsible stock, and use an Allen wrench or an Allen screwdriver bit to back out the screw at the upper rear of the pistol grip unit.

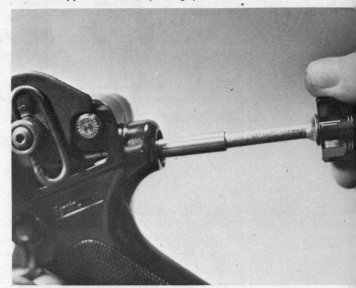

3. Remove the stock unit toward the rear.

4. Push out the large cross-pin at the lower rear of the receiver, and the smaller cross-pin at the front of the trigger group.

5. Remove the trigger group downward and toward the rear, tilting it slightly to clear the slide latch on the left.

6. Inside the lower edge of the receiver, depress the left shell stop, and move the action slide and bolt assembly forward out of the receiver. Lift the bolt off the action slide bars, and separate the bolt and slide piece.

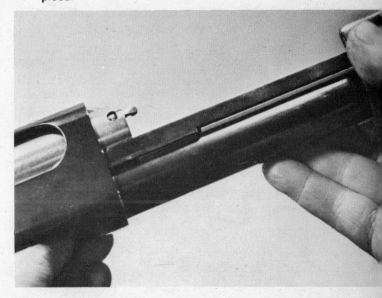

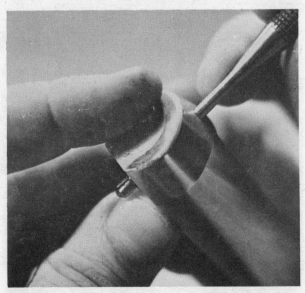

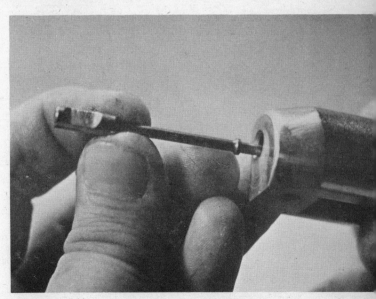

7. Restrain the firing pin, and drift out its vertical retaining pin downward.

8. Remove the firing pin from the rear of the bolt. The spring will be released from the underside of the bolt.

9. Remove the locking block from the underside of the bolt.

10. Insert a small sharp screwdriver between the extractor and its plunger, and depress the plunger toward the rear. Lift the extractor out of its recess in the bolt. **Caution:** *Keep the plunger and spring under control, and ease them out for removal toward the front.*

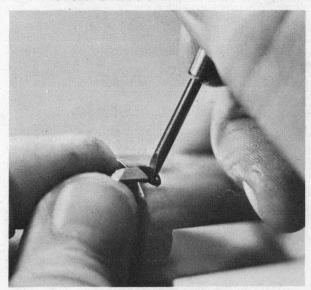

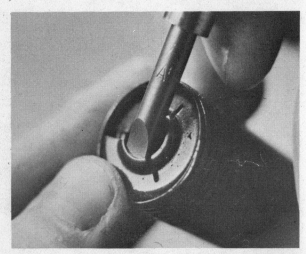

11. Insert a tool into the retainer at the front of the magazine tube, and pry it outward, moving the tool to lift it evenly. **Caution:** *The magazine spring will be released, so control it.* Remove the retainer, spring, and magazine follower. The ejector and its housing are riveted inside the left wall of the receiver, and should be removed only for repair. Replacement requires new rivets and a special tool. The right and left shell stops are staked in place in their recesses at the rear. If removal is necessary for repair, insert a sharp screwdriver to pry them inward, then remove them toward the rear.

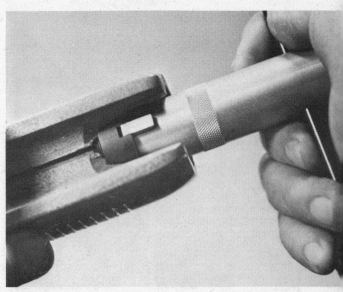

12. Use a B-Square Model 870 fore-end wrench or a piece of shop steel cut to fit, and unscrew the fore-end cap nut. Remove the action slide tube and bars toward the rear.

13. Restrain the carrier, and push out the carrier pivot, which is also the front group pin sleeve. Take care not to lose the lock spring at its end.

14. Release the spring tension slowly, and remove the carrier assembly upward and toward the front. Remove the carrier plunger and spring from their well on the right side. The carrier dog and its spacer plate are riveted on the right rear arm of the carrier, and should not be disturbed in normal takedown.

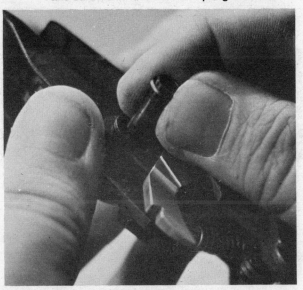

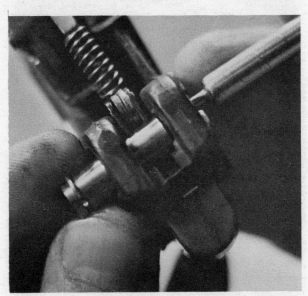

15. Restrain the hammer, pull the trigger, and ease the hammer down to fired position. Push out the rear group cross-pin sleeve toward the left, taking care not to lose the lock spring at its end.

16. Removal of the sleeve will allow the top of the trigger to move further toward the rear, relieving the tension of the sear and trigger spring. Detach the front of the spring from its stud on the back of the sear, and remove it upward.

17. Drift out the trigger cross-pin toward the left.

18. Remove the trigger assembly upward, turning it slightly to the left to clear the left connector. The two connectors are cross-pinned to the top of the trigger, and the pin is riveted. Remove this system only for repair.

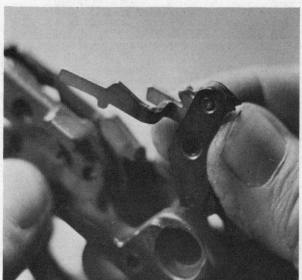

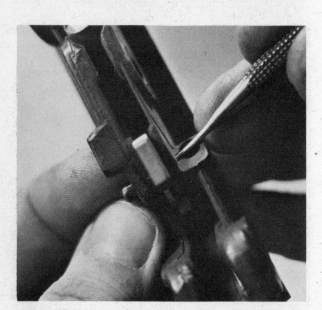

19. The sear cross-pin is accessible on the right side inside the carrier spring well. Angle a small drift punch to nudge it out toward the left.

20. Remove the sear upward.

21. The hammer and slide latch are pivoted and retained by the same cross-pin at the front of the trigger group, and the pin is riveted on the right side over a washer in a recess. This system should not be removed unless necessary for repair. If it is to be taken out, take care that the slide latch is not deformed during removal of the cross-pin, and restrain the hammer, as its plunger and spring will be released as the pin is removed. The slide latch spring will also be freed for removal.

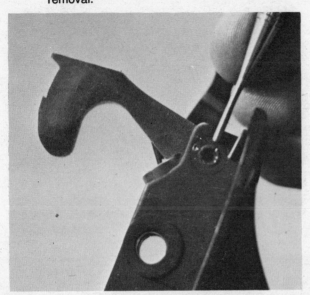

22. Hold a fingertip over the hole at the upper rear of the trigger group, and push out the safety spring cross-pin. Remove the safety spring upward. The safety detent ball will probably stay in the well.

23. Remove the safety toward either side. Insert a tool from the top to push the safety detent ball down into the safety tunnel, and remove it. Take care that this small steel ball is not lost.

Reassembly Tips:

1. When replacing the trigger assembly, be sure the forward tip of the left connector arm is positioned *above* the rear tail of the slide latch, as shown.

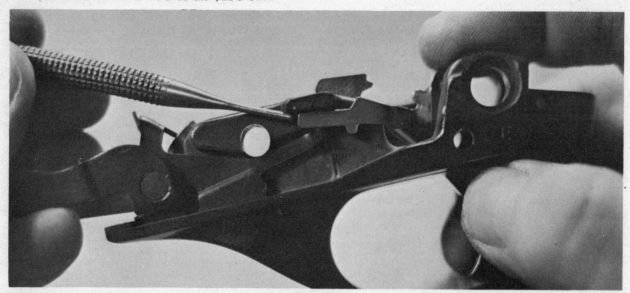

2. When replacing the carrier assembly, be sure the rear step of the carrier dog egages the carrier spring plunger correctly, as shown.

When replacing the firing pin in the bolt, insert the spring through the underside, and be sure the front of the spring enters its recess inside the front of the bolt.

When replacing the bolt and action slide assembly in the receiver, it is necessary to depress the right and left shell stops, in that order, as the assembly is moved back into place.

SECTION IV

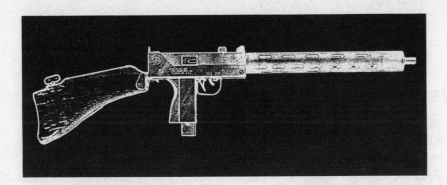

Pistol-caliber, semi-auto carbines often make a lot of sense in law enforcement applications. They are less expensive than submachine guns, and their use does not require the special training that should be given for full-auto pieces. Also, they *look* like submachine guns, and this psychological factor can be helpful in many situations. If the department is following the trend toward automatic pistols as duty sidearms, there is the added advantage of standardizing ammunition. Another plus is that they can be obtained and used without the extensive B.A.T.F. paperwork that the full-autos require.

COMMANDO MARK 45

Data:	Commando Mark 45 Carbine
Origin:	United States
Manufacturer:	Volunteer Enterprises, Inc. Knoxville, Tennessee
Cartridges:	45 ACP, 9 mm Parabellum
Magazine capacity:	30 rounds (others available)
Over-all length:	36⅛ inches
Barrel length:	16¼ inches
Weight:	8 pounds

Early production versions of the Commando Carbine, designated "Mark III," will have grip frames of alloy, while those of later manufacture, such as the one shown, have this section made of Valox, a space-age plastic. The internal mechanism, though, has remained basically unchanged, so the instructions will apply. As with all semi-auto carbines of this type, the firing mechanism has been designed to prevent any tampering in the direction of full-auto fire. The 9mm version, designated "Mark 9," is otherwise identical.

Disassembly:

1. With the magazine removed, pull the trigger to drop the striker to fired position. Remove the two Phillips screws in the forward underside of the buttstock, and detach the stock from the receiver.

2. Removal of the stock will expose a large slotted screw on the underside of the receiver (grip frame). Back out this screw and remove it.

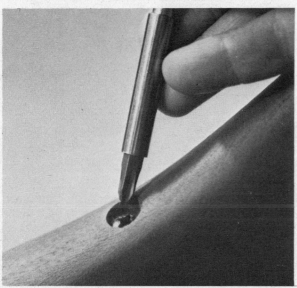

3. Slide the grip frame assembly toward the rear, to free it from the front underhook of the receiver, and take the assembly off downward.

4. Remove the feed throat (cartridge guide) from its recess in the top front of the grip frame. There is an aluminum plate press-fitted into the recess beneath the guide, and this is not routinely removed.

5. Unhook the front loop of the trigger spring from its hook at the rear tip of the sear activator lever. The spring is not removed at this time.

6. Gently pry the sear guide block from its recess on top of the grip frame, just behind the magazine well, and remove it.

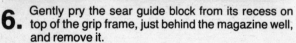

7. Drift out the roll pin which pivots and retains the sear and disconnector.

8. Remove the sear upward.

9. Remove the disconnector and the sear/disconnector spring upward.

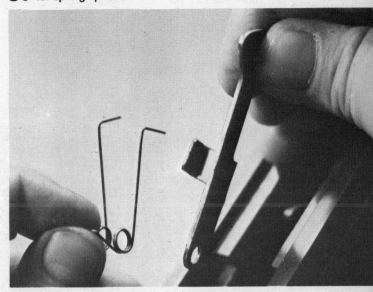

10. Drift out the roll pin which pivots and retains the trigger.

11. Remove the trigger and the attached sear activator lever upward. Note that the activator crosspin is staked in place, and is not routinely removed.

12. Tip the safety tension spring upward at the front, disengage it from the cross-pin at the rear, and remove it upward. If the trigger spring is also to be taken out, its cross-pin must be removed.

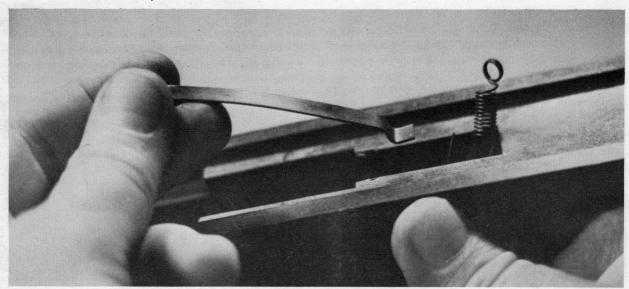

13. Turn the safety until the Phillips screw in its side points upward, remove the screw, and push the safety out to either side. Note that this screw is tightly fitted, and should be removed only if necessary.

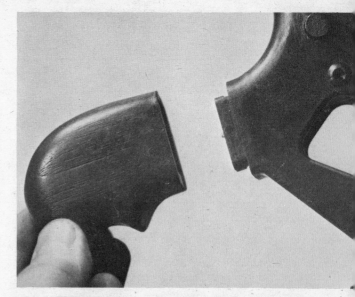

14. The pistol grip is retained by a single screw inside the receiver. During removal, do not attempt to take off the grip piece until the screw is fully backed out, as it is also threaded into the receiver.

15. The magazine catch and its coil spring are retained by a solid cross-pin which can be drifted out toward either side. As the catch is removed downward, take care that the spring isn't lost.

16. Use an Allen wrench or an Allen bit in the Magna-Tip screwdriver to remove the large screw inside the rear sight. This screw may be very tight, and may require that an Allen wrench be held in place and tapped with a hammer to start it. **Caution:** *This screw also retains the rear receiver endcap, which is under tension from the recoil spring, so restrain the cap as the screw is removed.*

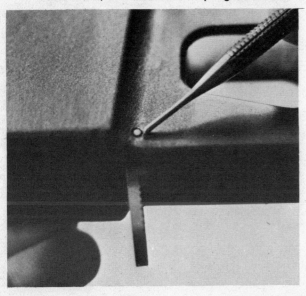

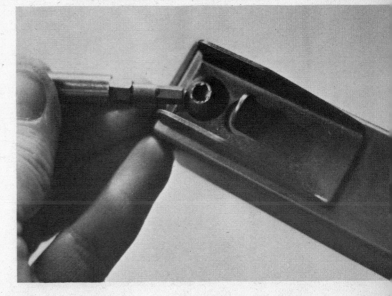

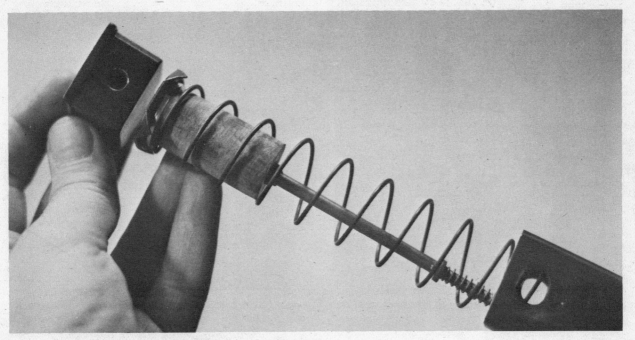

17. Slowly release the spring tension, and remove the buffer and guide unit and its attendant springs toward the rear. The springs are easily removed from the unit.

18. Move the bolt toward the rear until the bolt handle is aligned with the larger opening at the end of its track, and remove the handle toward the left.

19. Remove the bolt assembly from the rear of the receiver.

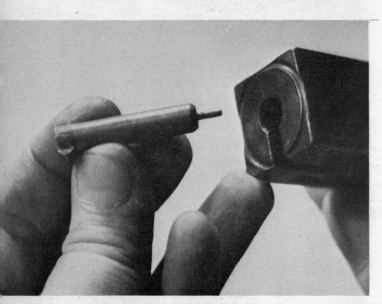

20. Remove the firing pin (striker) from the rear of the bolt.

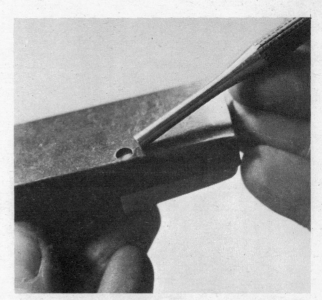

21. The extractor is retained by a large vertical pin on the right side of the bolt. Drive this pin upward until the extractor and its attached spring are freed for removal toward the right. *Do not attempt to drive the pin downward, or the spring will be damaged.*

22. The foregrip is retained by a slotted screw in the bottom of the grip, and is removed downward.

23. The front sight unit is retained by two Allen screws on its underside. After the screws are backed out, use a non-marring tool to nudge the unit off forward. The stop ring at the rear of the sight is also moved off toward the front.

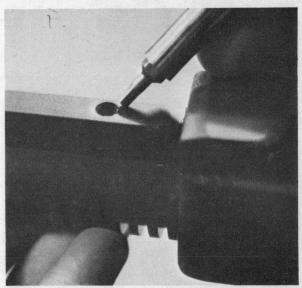

24. The finned cooling sleeve is retained by two Allen screws on its underside, and it is also moved off toward the front.

Reassembly Tips:

1. When replacing the trigger and attached sear activator lever, be sure the safety tension spring is depressed to place its forward end beneath the trigger cross-pin. Be sure the sear, disconnector, and their common spring are assembled as shown. In this view, the sear is tipped over forward to relieve spring tension during installation. Before replacement of the sear guide, the sear must be tipped over to the rear until it is caught by the activator.

2. When replacing the receiver endcap, be sure the bright steel insert nut is on the top, to match the threads of the Allen screw. The lower screw can be temporarily inserted to hold the endcap in place while the sight and upper screw are put in place.

DEMRO TAC-1

Data: Demro TAC-1 Carbine
Origin: United States
Manufacturer: Demro Products, Inc.
Manchester, Connecticut
Cartridge: 45 ACP
Magazine capacity: 30 rounds
Over-all length: 35¾ inches
Barrel length: 16⅞ inches
Weight: 8 pounds

The TAC-1 is unusual in having three separate safety systems. In addition to the manual safety lever and a grip safety, there is also a combination-lock three-number safety that can be set for up to one thousand combinations. As a means of preventing unauthorized use, this is a valuable asset. For use in cars or other close quarters, the stock is easily and quickly removable. A long sight radius aids accuracy.

Disassembly:

1. Remove the magazine, and set the bolt in the fired position. Depress the release button, and remove the buttstock.

2. Depress the latch lever at the rear of the receiver, and tip the barrel and receiver cover away from the frame.

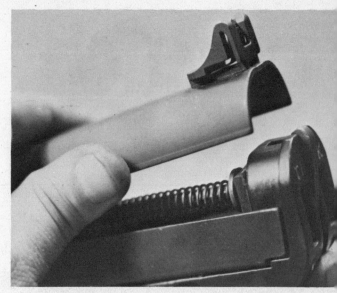

3. Lift the bolt assembly upward at the front, tilt it out to either side, and remove it toward the front. Keep the recoil spring under control.

4. Remove the recoil spring and its guide/ejector from the rear of the bolt.

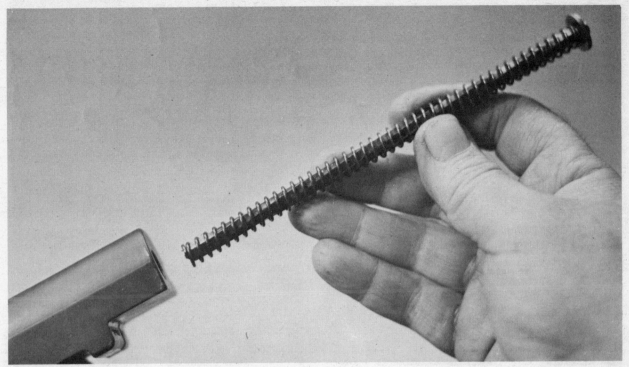

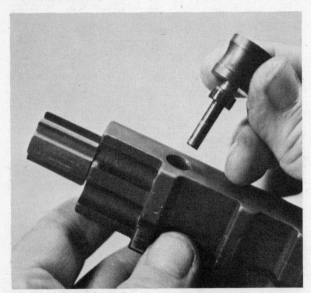

5. Remove the cocking handle from the side of the bolt.

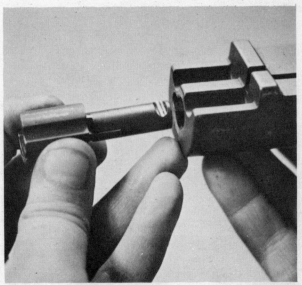

6. Remove the bolt head from the front of the bolt.

7. Remove the extractor from its recess on the side of the bolt head.

8. Remove the extractor spring from its well in the bolt head.

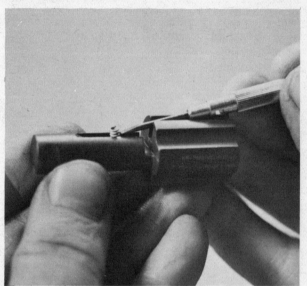

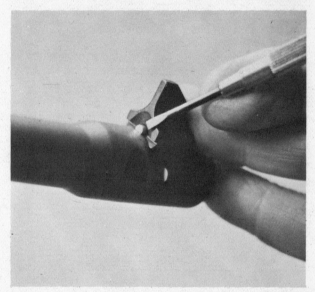

9. With the longer of the two stock mounting rods or a punch of appropriate size, push out the hinge pin at the front of the frame, and separate the barrel and cover unit from the frame.

10. Depress the plunger at the rear of the front sight, and slide the sight out toward either side. Take care that the small plunger and spring are not lost.

11. Remove the barrel toward the rear. If it is very tight, turning it while exerting rearward pressure will free it.

12. The fore-end piece is lifted straight upward for removal.

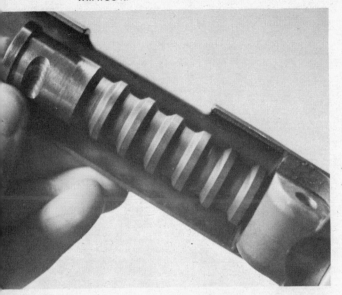

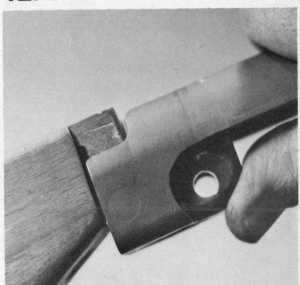

13. Turn the safety up to the vertical position, and remove it toward the left.

14. Lift the sub-frame at the front, until resistance is felt.

15. Move the sub-frame forward to clear its rear tabs from the frame at the rear, then remove it upward.

16. The cross-pins that retain the parts in the sub-frame are spot-welded in place, to prevent conversion to full-auto firing. For repairs to this unit, it must be returned to the factory.

17. Depress the grip safety, and move the combination lock slightly inward. Swing the safety arm upward, and detach the lock from its end.

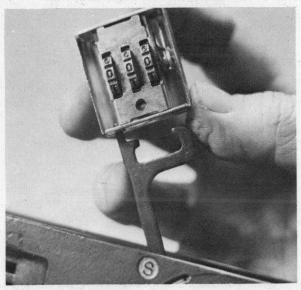

18. The magazine catch and its spring can now be moved straight upward and out of the frame.

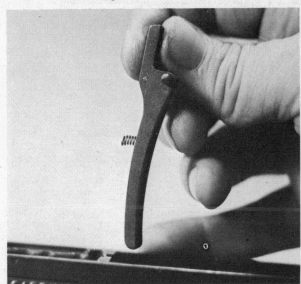

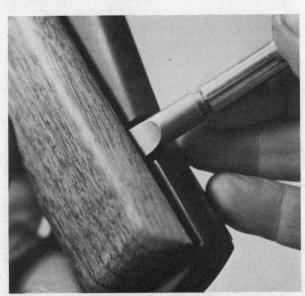

19. Insert a large screwdriver at the rear of the grip frame, just below the grip safety on the left, and pry the left grip panel outward.

20. Both grips can now be lifted off. They are retained by opposed ball-and-post plastic pads which snap into place.

21. Push out the forward grip safety cross-pin.

22. Push out the lower grip safety cross-pin.

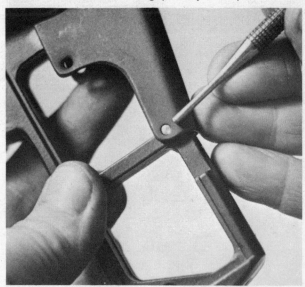

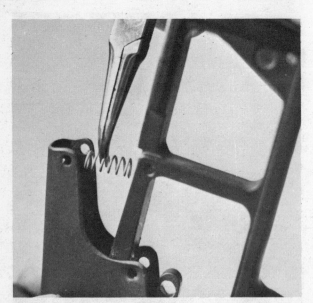

23. Move the grip safety slighty to the rear, and remove the grip safety spring from inside it.

24. Move the grip safety downward, then turn it around the backstrap for removal.

25. Drift out the cross-pin that retains the grip safety lever.

26. Remove the grip safety lever and the attached safety bar upward. The bar is retained by a roll pin which is riveted on both sides, and this should be removed only for repair purposes.

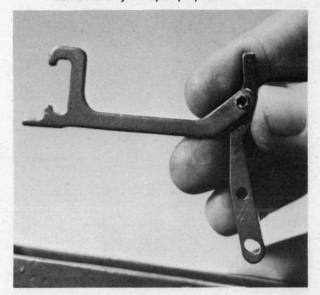

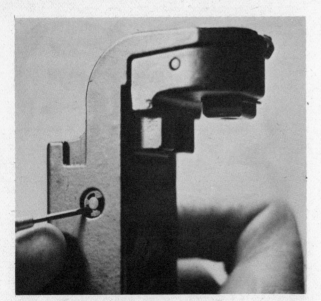

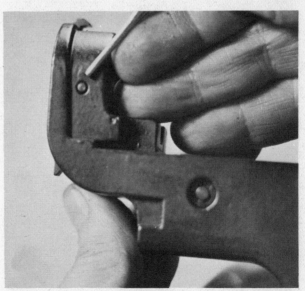

27. The stock latch and its spring are retained on the right side of the frame by a C-clip. For removal, the button must be depressed to allow clearance for detachment of the C-clip. The button and spring are then removed toward the left.

28. The cover latch at the rear is retained by a cross-pin, and the latch and its spring are removed toward the rear.

Reassembly Tips:

1. When replacing the bolt head in the bolt, align the bolt head groove with the ejector tunnel, and depress the rear of the extractor as the bolt head is pushed into place.

INGRAM SM11-A1

Data:	SM11-A1 Carbine
Origin:	United States
Manufacturer:	RPB Industries, Inc. Atlanta, Georgia
Cartridge:	380 ACP
Magazine capacity:	16 and 32 rounds
Over-all length:	28¾ inches
Barrel length:	16¼ inches
Weight:	6 pounds

Based on the original Ingram submachine gun design, this gun was originally produced by Military Armament Corporation as the MAC-10 and MAC-11, designations by which they are still popularly known. It addition to the 380 ACP chambering, they are also available in 45 ACP and 9mm Parabellum. The semi-auto versions of each caliber have the same mechanisms as the gun shown here. To prevent conversion to full-auto, the components of the sear, trigger, and disconnector system are semi-permanently installed.

Disassembly:

1. With the magazine removed and the bolt forward, push the large cross-pin at the lower front of the receiver out toward the right and remove it.

2. Lift the barrel and receiver assembly at the front, then remove it forward.

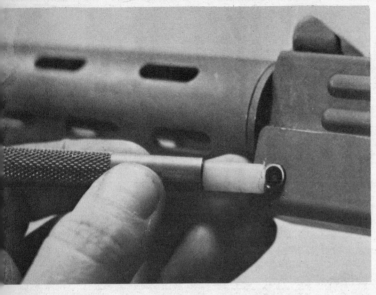

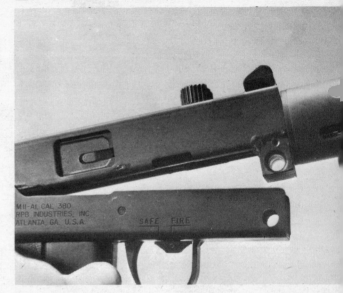

3. Move the bolt toward the rear until the bolt handle is aligned with the larger opening at the rear of its track, and pull the bolt handle off upward. Remove the bolt assembly toward the rear.

4. The bolt spring assembly, which includes the spring guide and ejector, is best left attached to the bolt in normal takedown. If removal is necessary, compress the spring slightly to expose a small cross-pin in the front tip of the guide. Drive out the pin, guide, and spring, and the ejector assembly will be released for removal toward the rear. **Caution:** *The spring is compressed. Ease it out.*

5. The extractor is retained by a vertical roll pin on the right side of the bolt. Drift out the pin upward, and remove the extractor and its coil spring toward the right.

6. The bolt handle spring and plunger are retained by a small vertical roll pin at the front edge of the bolt. Drive the pin upward, and remove the spring and plunger toward the front. **Caution:** *This is a strong little spring, under tension. Release it carefully.*

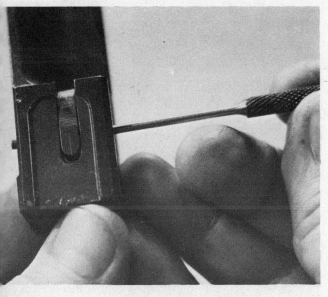

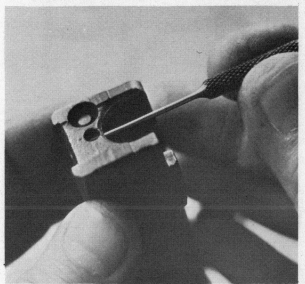

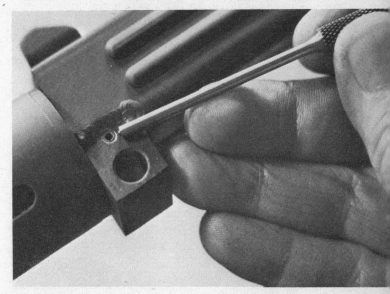

7. Removal of the cooling jacket requires a special twin-lug wrench, and in normal takedown it is best left in place. If removal is necessary, this unit can be turned by inserting a rod section or a large drift punch in one of the recesses, and tapping its side with a small hammer, counter-clockwise (front view).

8. The barrel is threaded into the receiver at the rear, and is also secured by a large roll pin through the receiver. Since rear projection of the barrel is adjustable, and its meeting with the bolt face critical, barrel removal is definitely not recommended.

9. The principal parts of the firing mechanism in the lower frame are semi-permanently installed to prevent full-auto conversion, but removal of the springs for replacement is possible. The trigger cross-pin is retained by two C-clips on the left side. Carefully lift the clips off upward, being careful not to lose them.

10. Push out the trigger pin toward the left.

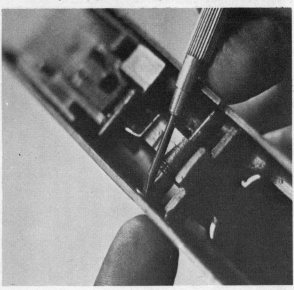

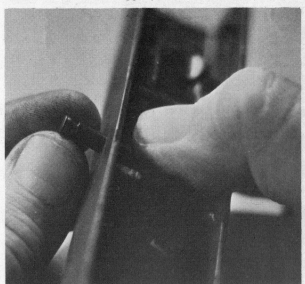

11. Move the trigger forward, disengage the trigger/disconnector spring from the two parts, and remove the spring upward.

12. Insert a small screwdriver through the hole in the top of the sear to slightly compress the sear spring. Tip the spring toward the rear, and remove it.

13. The safety is retained by a small roll pin that crosses the safety button on the outside. When the pin is drifted out, the button is removed downward, and the safety block and its spring and plunger are removed upward.

14. Remove the screw in the back center of the hand-grip/magazine housing.

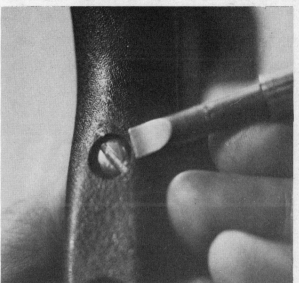

15. Remove the rear section of the hand-grip toward the rear. It may be tight, and require gentle prying at top and bottom to free it. Take care not to lose the magazine catch spring.

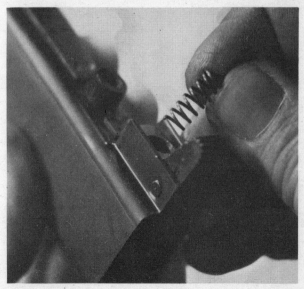

16. Remove the spring from the back of the magazine catch.

Reassembly Tips:

17. Push out the magazine catch cross-pin, and remove the catch downward.

1. When replacing the combination trigger and disconnector spring, be sure the front lower hook goes beneath the forward arm of the trigger, and the front upper hook beneath the left arm of the disconnector, as shown.

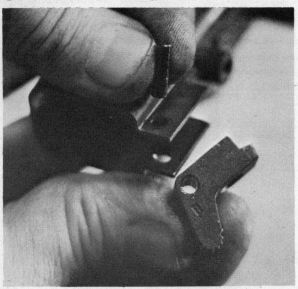

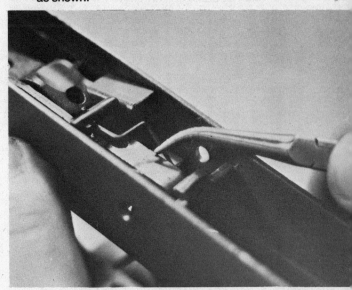

The rear loop of the trigger/disconnector spring must go behind and below the rear of the trigger. When inserting the cross-pin, exert downward pressure on the trigger while guiding the right tip of the pin into its hole in the receiver. Be sure both C-clips are fully snapped in place on the left side after the pin is installed.

18. Remove the large screw at the front of the stock bracket, and take off the buttstock toward the rear. The location of this screw, behind the magazine housing, may require an angle-tip or offset screwdriver.

THOMPSON 1927 A-1

Data: Thompson 1927 A-1 Carbine
Origin: United States
Manufacturer: Auto-Ordnance Corp.
West Hurley, New York
Cartridge: 45 ACP
Magazine capacity: 20 rounds (others available)
Over-all length: 37¾ inches
Barrel length: 17 inches
Weight: 11½ pounds

Just before the introduction of the re-designed Model 1928 Thompson submachinegun, the company briefly made a semi-auto version, the Model 1927. The Auto-Ordnance Corporation, now a subsidiary of Numrich Arms, has re-created this gun as the Model 1927 A-1, in "standard" and "deluxe" versions. These guns are quite different in some mechanical aspects from the original guns, as the instructions will indicate. The "standard" version is the one shown.

Disassembly:

1. With the magazine removed and the bolt forward, pull the trigger to drop the striker. Depress the takedown button at the lower rear of the receiver, and slide the buttstock and grip frame unit toward the rear. When it stops, pull the trigger, and the unit can then be moved a short distance further.

2. Insert a tool at the rear to depress the sear, and remove the buttstock and grip frame unit toward the rear.

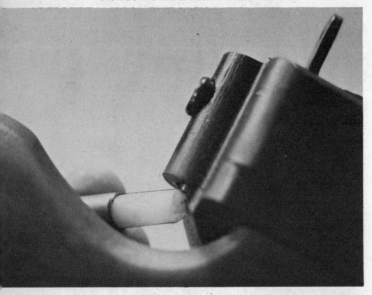

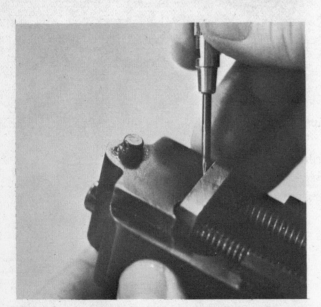

3. Invert the receiver, and use a small screwdriver to lever the buffer and recoil spring guide unit forward and outward. **Caution:** *The springs are under tension, so keep the unit under control.*

4. Grip the unit firmly, tip it outward, and remove it toward the rear.

5. Remove the striker spring and guide from the rear of the receiver.

6. Move the bolt to the rear, until the bolt handle is aligned with the larger opening at the end of its track, and remove the bolt handle from the top of the receiver.

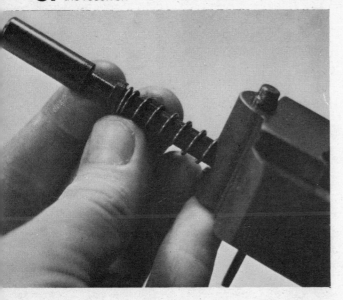

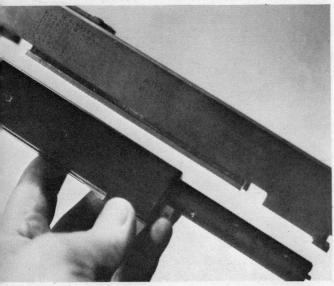

7. Remove the bolt from the bottom of the receiver.

8. Remove the cylindrical hammer from the rear of the bolt.

9. Drift out the rear firing pin (striker) retaining pin toward the right. Drift out the forward striker retaining pin toward the right. Note that the small cross-pin in the forward section of the bolt is only a guide, and does not have to be removed.

10. Remove the striker from the rear of the bolt.

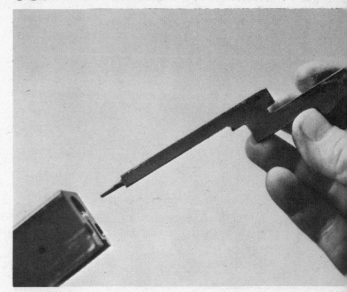

11. Insert a screwdriver vertically under the extractor beak, and lift it just enough to clear its underlug from the recess in the bolt, then lever it forward out of the bolt. **Caution:** *If the extractor is lifted too much, it can be deformed or broken.*

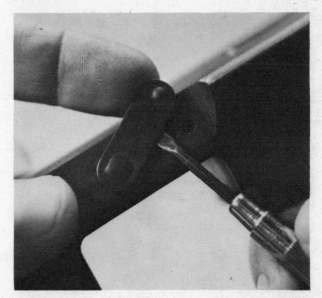

12. To remove the ejector, use a screwdriver to lift its rear tail, just enough to clear its locking lug, then unscrew the ejector counter-clockwise (left side view) and remove it. Avoid over-lifting of the spring tail, and insert a card to prevent marring of the receiver as the part is turned.

13. The takedown button is held in its well at the rear of the receiver only by the friction of its coil spring, and can be easily pulled out.

14. The fore-end is released by removal of a single mounting screw, and this applies also if the gun has the vertical fore-grip. The mounting bar is press-fitted into the receiver, and is not removed in normal takedown. The barrel is screw-mounted in the receiver, and should not be removed unless it is absolutely necessary.

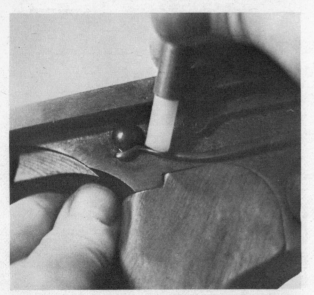

15. Use a non-marring tool to depress the lower arm of the pivot plate on the right side of the grip frame, detaching it from the cross-piece of the safety lever, and push the safety toward the left. This is most easily done with the safety in mid-position. Remove the safety toward the left.

16. Push simultaneously on the two pivot plate posts on the left side, moving the plate toward the right.

17. When the left tip of the rear post has cleared the disconnector, the disconnector can be removed upward.

18. Remove the pivot plate and its attached posts toward the right. Take care not to exert any force on the spring-tempered lower arm of the plate during removal.

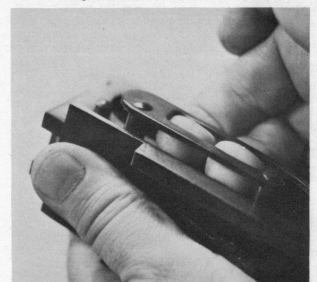

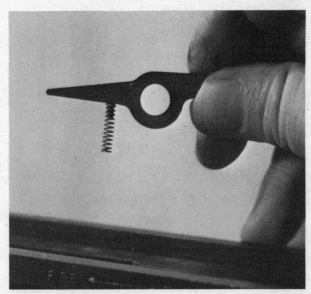

19. Remove the sear and its spring upward.

20. Remove the bolt latch and its spring upward.

21. Remove the trigger assembly upward. The sear trip is mounted on the trigger by a riveted cross-pin, and is not removed in normal takedown.

22. Remove the bolt latch activator upward.

23. Push the magazine catch upward beyond its normal release position, and push the right tip of its pivot toward the left. Remove the magazine catch toward the left. The catch spring is mounted on the pivot, and is easily removed.

24. The buttstock is retained by two large screws in its forward underside, and the pistol grip piece is retained by a single vertical screw. Both are removed downward.

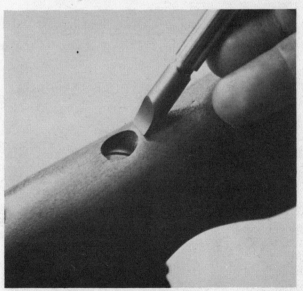

Reassembly Tips:

1. When replacing the magazine catch, be sure the outer end of the catch spring is in its hole on the inner face of the catch lever, and see that the inner tip of the spring enters its recess in the grip frame as the catch is started into place.

2. Note that the front cross-pin on the pivot plate is slightly longer than the rear one, so the bolt latch activator and trigger must be inserted into the grip frame first. Remember that the front tip of the bolt latch must rest beneath the rear extension of the activator. The disconnector is inserted last. The parts are shown in their proper order.

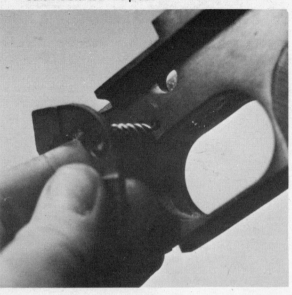

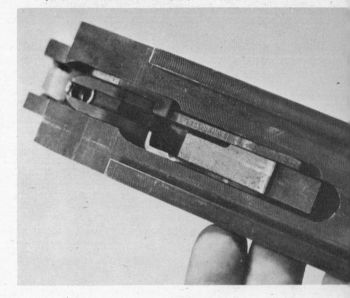

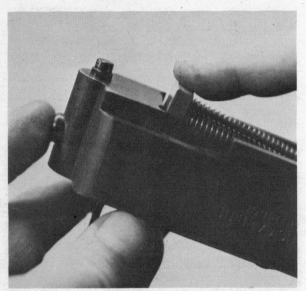

3. When replacing the buffer and recoil spring guide unit, the striker spring guide must be depressed to align its collar with the slot in the buffer plate, as shown.

UZI SEMI-AUTO

Data:	Uzi Carbine
Origin:	Israel
Manufacturer:	Israel Military Industries Tel Aviv
Cartridge:	9mm Luger
Magazine capacity:	25 rounds
Over-all length:	31½ inches (stock extended)
Barrel length:	16.1 inches
Weight:	8.85 pounds

The original selective-fire version of the Uzi was designed by Major Uziel Gal around 1950, with the main elements of design borrowed from the Czech ZK-476 submachine gun. In 1980, Major Gal and IMI engineers designed a semi-auto carbine version of the Uzi, with dimensions that allow it to be sold in the U.S. This gun fires with the bolt closed, and has a separate firing pin.

Disassembly:

1. With the magazine removed and the striker in the fired position, depress the barrel retaining nut catch, and unscrew the nut until it can be moved forward on the barrel. Remove the barrel toward the front.

2. Exert downward pressure on the receiver cover, and depress the receiver cover latch, located just below the front of the rear sight. Allow the receiver cover to move upward at the rear. Lift the rear of the cover, and remove it upward and toward the rear.

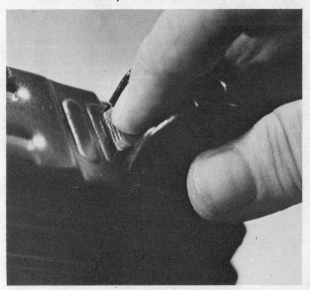

3. The cocking knob return spring is easily detached from its hook on the cocking plate. For complete removal, the front loop of the spring must be flexed and rotated out of its attachment hole. The knob and track cover plate are attached to the cocking plate by a large vertical screw, and the inside tip of this screw is semi-riveted. Removal should be done only for repair.

4. Be certain that the striker is in the fired position. Move the front of the bolt upward, exerting slight rearward pressure to control the spring tension. Remove the bolt assembly upward and toward the front.

5. Remove the striker and firing pin assembly from the rear of the bolt.

6. The firing pin is retained on the striker block by a vertical roll pin which is drifted out upward, and the firing pin is removed toward the front. The striker spring is retained on the guide at the rear by constricted coils at its forward end, and removal requires that these coils be pried out of their groove toward the rear. In normal takedown, leave it in place.

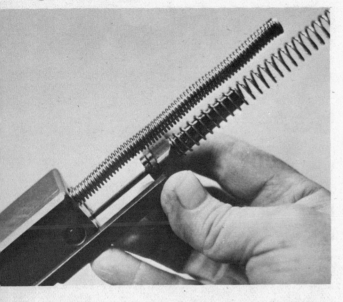

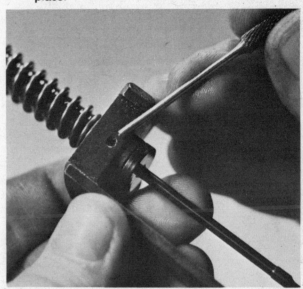

7. Remove the recoil spring assembly from the rear of the bolt. Note that this is a captive spring, its ends retained on the guide by riveted washers. The spring unit is reversible. The extractor is retained by a cross-pin with a split tempered end. Use a nylon drift punch to start the pin toward the left.

8. Use a drift of smaller diameter to push the pin out toward the left for removal.

9. The same drift can be used to push the extractor forward out of the bolt.

10. Push out the grip frame retainer toward the left.

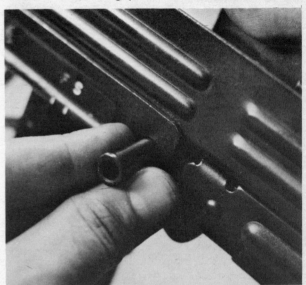

12. Depress the grip safety and pull the trigger. The sear will flip over forward, easing the tension of its spring.

11. Tip the grip frame down at the rear, and remove it.

13. Remove the two cross-screws at the rear of the pistol-grip panels, and take off the panels toward each side. When the grip panels are removed, the grip safety will move to the rear, beyond its normal rear position. Flex the grip safety spring out of its recesses, and remove it.

14. Keeping the grip safety at the rear, push the sear pivot out toward the right, and remove it.

15. Remove the sear and its attached spring, and the trip limit block, upward. The spring is easily detached from the sear.

16. Tip the sear trip on the front of the trigger over forward, and insert a tool to push each of the forward arms of the trigger spring downward and toward the side, detaching them from the trip. **Caution:** *Keep fingertips clear, as the spring ends will snap over to the rear, relieving some of the trigger spring tension.*

17. Keeping the grip safety at the rear, restrain the trigger assembly and push the trigger pivot out toward the right.

18. Remove the trigger and its spring, and the safety cam block, upward. The sear trip is cross-pinned at the upper front of the trigger, and the pin is riveted. This should not be removed except for repair.

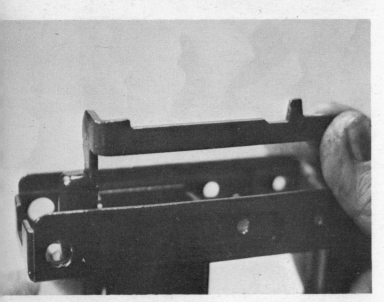

19. Move the grip safety back to the front, and remove it upward.

20. Set the manual safety halfway between its two positions, and use a fingertip at the front and a tool at the rear to lift its internal bar upward.

21. Remove the internal bar upward, and take off the safety button toward the left.

22. Insert a small screwdriver into the safety slot from below, and flex the front of the safety positioning spring toward the left, then upward for removal from the top.

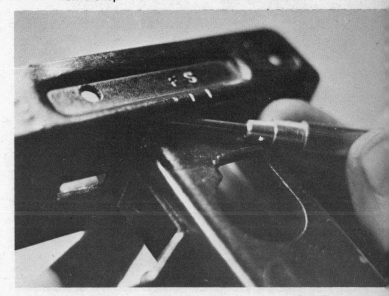

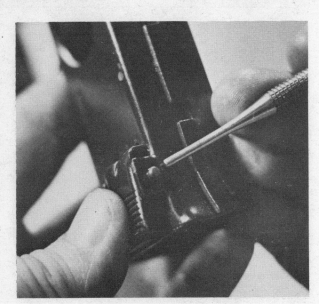

23. The magazine catch and its spring are retained on the grip frame by a cross-pin. **Caution:** *The spring is strong, and it is compressed, so control it.* If removal is not necessary for repair, it's best to leave the catch system in place, as reassembly may require a slave pin.

24. The handguard is retained by two cross-screws that are threaded into slotted nuts on the opposite side. A twin-point screwdriver is best to stabilize the slotted nuts, but this can also be done by holding a very small screwdriver firmly in one side of the slot while the screw is removed. Since removal of the handguard panels does not give access to any parts, they are best left in place. If it becomes necessary to remove the barrel retaining nut latch and its spring, this can be done by removing the front sight, using the adjustment tool.

25. The rear sight is also retained by a cross-screw with a slotted nut which must be stabilized during removal. Restrain the rear sight as the screw is taken out, and remove the sight and its spring upward. Also restrain the receiver cover latch and its spring, as they will be released by removal of the sight.

26. With an Allen wrench or an Allen screwdriver bit of the proper size, remove the stock mounting screw and take off the buttstock assembly toward the rear. A roll pin retains the stock latch button and its spring in the stock base. The stock components are cross-pinned and riveted in place, and this system is not routinely disassembled.

Reassembly Tips:

1. When replacing the sear assembly, note that the loop of the sear spring must rest against the inside front of the grip frame, as shown. Note that the sear and trigger pivots have recesses near their right tips to clear the grip safety bar, and the right tips of the pins are slotted to aid orientation. Remember that the grip safety must be fully to the rear as the pivots are installed.

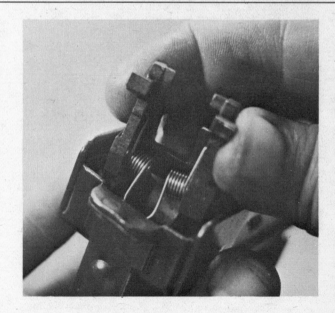

3. When replacing the extractor, insert it from the rear, and align its screw-slot horizontally with the small arrow on the rear of the bolt, with the half-slot downward. Be sure the inner groove is properly aligned with the cross-hole in the bolt, and insert the retaining pin toward the right.

2. This photo shows the sear and trigger systems in their proper order in the grip frame.

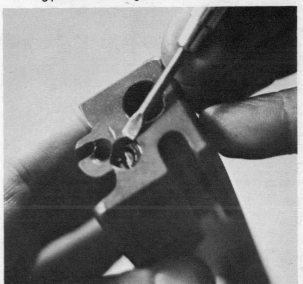

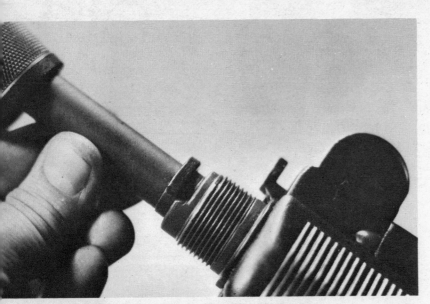

4. When replacing the barrel, be sure the flats of the interrupted ring engage their mating surfaces on the barrel bushing in the receiver.

WILKINSON TERRY

Data:	Terry Carbine
Origin:	United States
Manufacturer:	Wilkinson Arms Covina, California
Cartridge:	9mm Luger (Parabellum)
Magazine capacity:	31 rounds
Over-all length:	28¾ inches
Barrel length:	16³⁄₁₆ inches
Weight:	7⅛ pounds

There was an earlier version of this gun, not made by Wilkinson, which was marketed as the PJK M68. This gun was of lesser quality than the Terry, and was not mechanically identical, although similar in appearance. The instructions given here apply only to the genuine Terry Carbine, as made by Wilkinson.

Disassembly:

1. Remove the magazine, and cycle the action to cock the hammer. Unscrew the knurled barrel retaining nut at the front of the receiver (counter-clockwise, front view), and remove the barrel assembly toward the front. If necessary, the flash hider can also be unscrewed from the muzzle, allowing removal of the barrel nut forward. If this is done, take care not to lose the twin half-rings at the rear of the flash hider.

2. With an Allen wrench, or an Allen bit in the Magna-Tip screwdriver, remove the vertical Allen screws at the front and rear of the grip frame. If the fore-end piece is also to be taken off, it is retained by two Allen screws of the same size. Remove the grip frame downward.

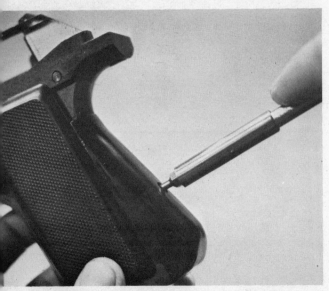

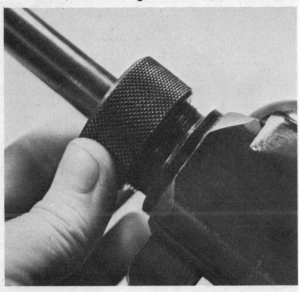

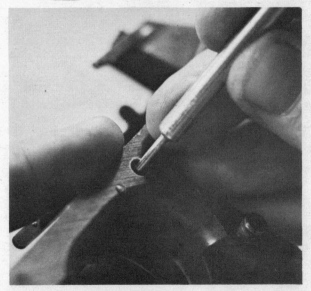

3. Remove the Allen screw in the backstrap of the grip frame, and remove the backstrap toward the rear. The grip side panels can now be lifted off the grip frame.

4. Hold a fingertip over the hole on top of the grip frame just above the safety, on the left side, and push the safety out toward the right. Use a drift punch near the size of the safety, to prevent loss of the safety detent ball.

5. Carefully withdraw the drift punch, and remove the safety detent ball and spring from their recess in the grip frame. If the spring sticks in the hole, a small screwdriver can be used to lift it out.

6. Removal of the safety will have partially released the cartridge guide, or feed ramp. Drifting out the small pin that crosses the lower end of the guide will allow its removal upward. All pins must be drifted out toward the right.

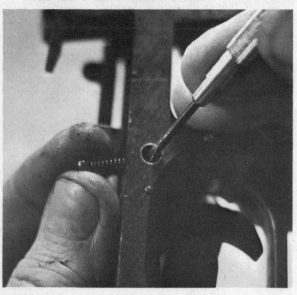

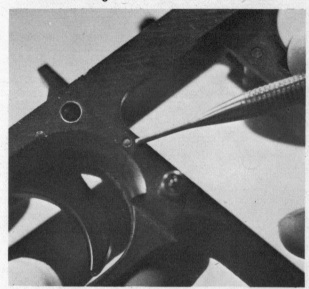

7. Restrain the trigger and trigger bar (disconnector) at the top of the grip frame, and drift out the trigger cross-pin toward the right.

8. Remove the trigger assembly upward. Note that the trigger insert, or connector, is retained in the trigger by a cross-pin. In normal takedown this is best left in place. The trigger spring is easily removed from its well in front of the trigger.

9. Depress the trigger bar (disconnector) at the rear to clear the sear wing, and move it forward until it can be lifted out of its guide at the front. As the bar is moved, control the rear disconnector spring beneath its rear tip to prevent loss. Remove the small spring inside the guide at the front. The guide is press-fitted into the grip frame, and should not be removed.

10. Remove the rear disconnector spring from its well at the rear.

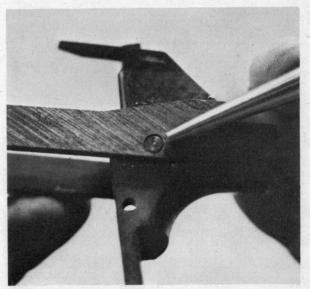

11. Restrain the hammer, trip the sear, and gently lower the hammer to fired position. Restrain the sear, inside the magazine well, and drift out the sear cross-pin toward the right. Note the position of the sear spring before removal. **Caution:** *The sear spring will be released when the pin is removed, so control it.* Remove the sear and its spring forward, into the magazine well.

12. Drift the hammer cross-pin toward the right, just enough to clear the ejector. Restrain the hammer, as the ejector is also the hammer stop.

13. While holding the hammer, remove the ejector upward.

14. Slowly allow the hammer to tip over forward into the magazine well, relieving the tension of its spring, and drift the hammer pin out toward the right.

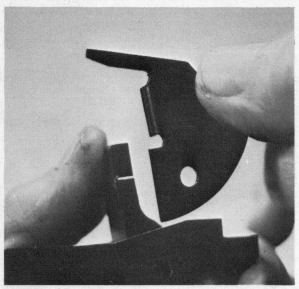

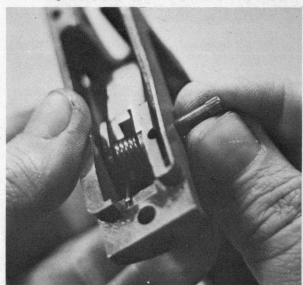

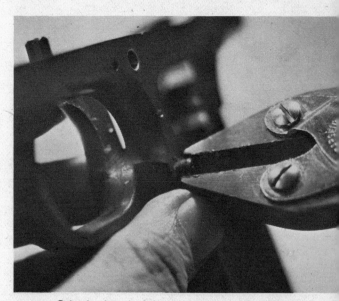

15. Remove the hammer and its spring from the top of the grip frame.

16. Grip the head of the magazine catch with non-marring smooth-jawed pliers, and unscrew the catch button from the cross-shaft of the catch (counter-clockwise, left side view). Remove the button and spring toward the left, and the magazine catch toward the right.

17. Remove the Allen screw on the underside at the forward end of the buttstock.

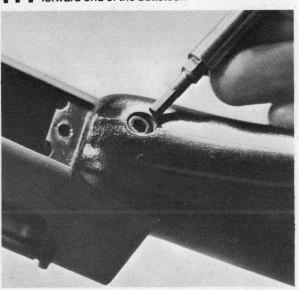

18. A hole is provided at the top of the rubber butt-plate that will allow a slim, long-shanked screwdriver to reach the slotted screw in the front interior of the stock. The buttplate can also be easily pulled out to allow direct acess to the screw. Remove the screw, and take off the buttstock toward the rear. It should be noted that removal of the stock at this point is not necessary to further disassembly, and the remainder of takedown can be done with the stock in place.

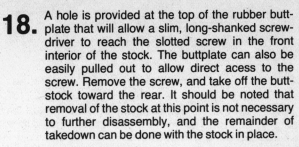

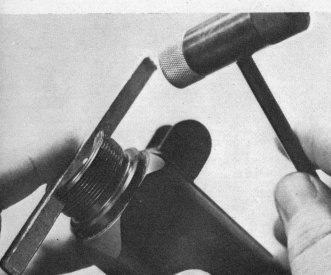

19. If you do not have an original Terry disassembly kit, use a piece of bar stock of suitable size, such as the aluminum piece shown, to engage the slots at the front of the barrel sleeve. The sleeve is then unscrewed from the receiver counter-clockwise (front view). If it is very tight, tap the end of the bar with a small hammer. An alternate method is to grip the bar in a vise, and turn the receiver. Note that the barrel timing pin is press-fitted in the sleeve, and is not removed. The rear receiver endpiece also should not be disturbed.

20. With an Allen wrench of the proper size, unscrew and remove the bolt handle, counter-clockwise (left side view). **Caution:** *Restrain the bolt as the handle is removed, as it will be released.* Note that the bolt handle may be tightly fitted, and may require that an Allen wrench be tapped with a hammer to free it.

21. Remove the bolt assembly from the front of the receiver. The twin recoil springs and their guides are easily removed from the rear of the bolt.

22. The extractor is retained by a vertical pin on the right side of the bolt, and the pin is drifted out downward.

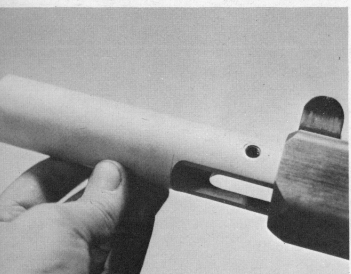

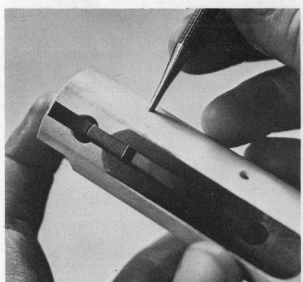

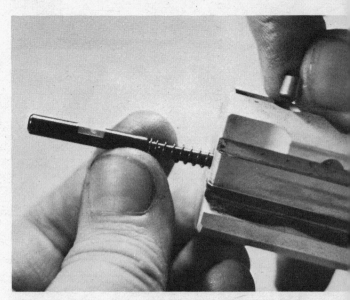

23. Gently lift the front of the extractor to free it, then remove it toward the right.

24. Removal of the extractor will expose the firing pin retaining button at the rear. Depress and restrain the firing pin at the rear, and tap the bolt with a nylon hammer to jar the button out of its recess. Remove the firing pin and its spring toward the rear.

25. The front sight is retained by twin Allen screws, and is taken off upward.

26. To remove the rear sight, first loosen the vertical adjustment screw on the left side, and slide the upper portion of the sight off forward and upward.

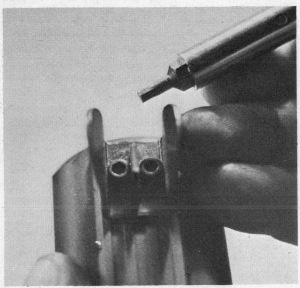

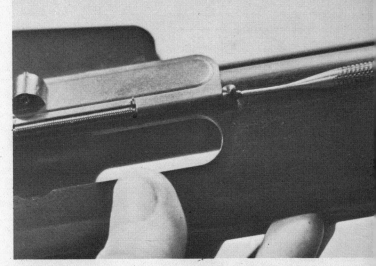

27. Removal of the sight slide will expose the rear retaining screw. Remove both Allen screws, and take off the sight and its protective bracket upward.

28. The ejection port cover can be removed by drifting out its hinge pin toward the rear. This pin is tightly fitted in the loops on the cover, so be sure the rear hinge post on the receiver is well supported during removal. Note that the cover spring will be released as the pin is removed, so control it. Unless removal is necessary for repair, the cover should be left in place. Also note that the cover latch plunger and spring are retained by riveting of the plunger tail, and the same advice applies to these parts.

Reassembly Tips:

1. When replacing the bolt in the receiver, be sure the bolt is in proper alignment, and insert a tool at the rear to insure that the twin recoil spring guides enter their recesses in the receiver end-piece. As the bolt is moved to the rear, be sure that the springs do not twist and deform.

2. When replacing the sear and sear spring, start the sear pin into the sear, then insert a drift from the opposite side and push the spring into place, holding it with the tip of the drift until the pin is driven into place. If this proves difficult, a slave pin can be used.

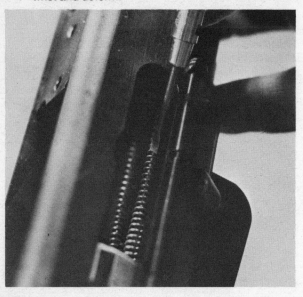

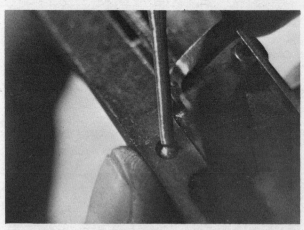

3. When replacing the trigger bar (disconnector), place it in its slot in the front guide, and use a tool to depress the rear spring while sliding the bar into place at the rear.

4. When replacing the safety system, remember that the twin grooves on the safety go on the left side. Being sure the cartridge guide is in upright position, insert the safety from the right. Move the safety until its left tip is even with the detent spring hole, then place the spring and ball in position, and while holding a fingertip over the safety opening on the left side, use a drift to compress the ball and spring, and push the safety toward the left into place.

When replacing the barrel, be sure the slot in the collar, midway on the barrel, mates with the locator or timing pin in the barrel sleeve before tightening the barrel retaining nut.

SECTION V

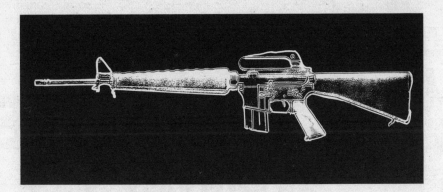

While the true rifle in police work is mainly in the province of the Special Weapons And Tactics people, several of the light military-style pieces are seeing a lot of use as patrol car guns, in the same role as the shotguns and pistol-caliber carbines. These guns are usually chambered for the 5.56mm military round, but a few of them are available in 7.62mm NATO (308 Winchester) chambering. Here, again, the appearance of the guns, and their similarity to the full-auto military versions, can be a valuable deterrent.

ARMALITE AR-180

Data:	Armalite AR-180
Origin:	United States
Manufacturer:	Armalite, Incorporated Costa Mesa, California
Cartridge:	223 Rem. (5.56mm)
Magazine capacity:	5 and 20 rounds
Over-all length:	38 inches
Barrel length:	18¼ inches
Weight:	6½ pounds

This semi-auto-only version of the AR-18 has a slight external resemblance to the U.S. M-16 and the AR-15, but it is very different mechanically. In several ways, it is superior to that basic design. It is of simpler construction, and is easier to operate and field strip. In addition to the Armalite production, the AR-180 has also been manufactured under license in England, Netherlands, and Japan.

Disassembly:

1. If the gun has an Armalite telescopic sight, push the scope base latch toward the left, and move the scope and base toward the rear until it stops. A spring inside the base will be compressd.

2. Move the scope and base straight upward, and when the base has cleared its track on top of the receiver, the scope assembly will be forced off toward the front.

3. Remove the magazine, and cycle the action to cock the internal hammer. Set the safety in the on-safe position. Depress the receiver latch plunger, and push the receiver latch forward. Its upper projection will enter the rear sight mount.

4. Keeping the latch depressed, tilt the rear of the receiver upward. **Caution:** *Keep a firm grip on the latch, as it is the rear base of the compressed recoil spring assembly.*

5. Slowly release the spring tension, and remove the recoil spring assembly from the rear of the receiver.

6. Move the bolt back to align the bolt handle with the larger opening at the end of its track, and remove the bolt handle toward the right.

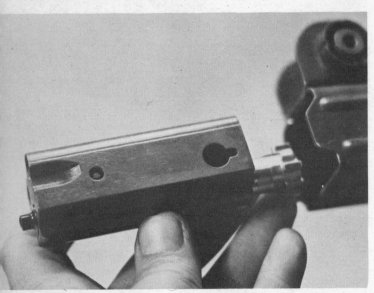

7. Remove the bolt assembly toward the rear.

8. Depress and hold the firing pin, and push the firing pin retaining cross-pin out toward the left and remove it.

9. Remove the firing pin and its spring toward the rear.

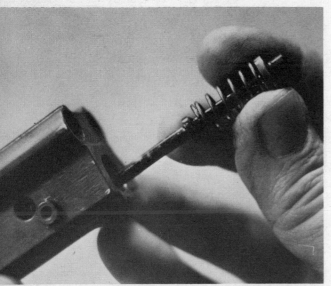

10. Remove the bolt cam pin toward the left.

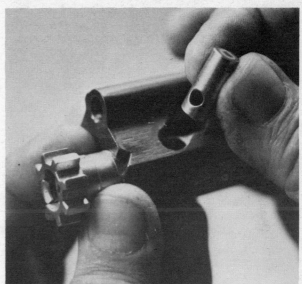

11. Remove the bolt from the front of the carrier.

12. Restrain the extractor, and push out the extractor cross-pin toward either side.

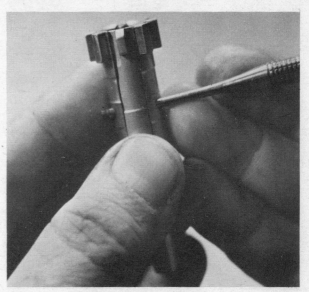

13. Remove the extractor and its spring from the bolt.

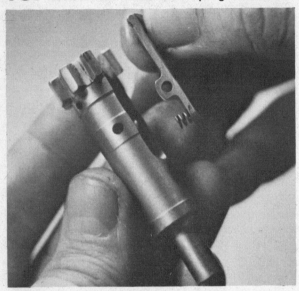

14. The ejector is retained by a small roll pin at the front of the bolt. Restrain the ejector against the tension of its spring, and drift out the roll pin. Remove the ejector and its spring toward the front.

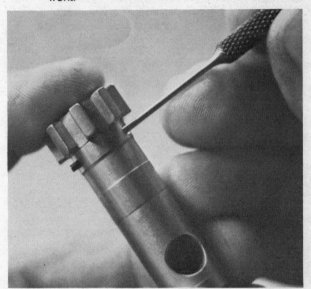

15. Push out the hinge pin at the front of the receiver toward the right, and separate the grip frame and buttstock unit from the receiver.

16. Removal of the recoil spring unit will have released the upper handguard. Tip it upward at the rear, and remove it.

17. Move the gas piston rod toward the rear, fully compressing its spring, and remove the connector toward the rear, tilting it toward the side.

18. Slowly release the spring tension, moving the gas piston rod forward and tilting it toward the side for removal, along with its spring.

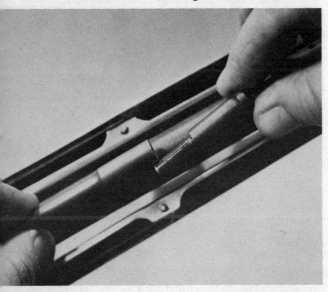

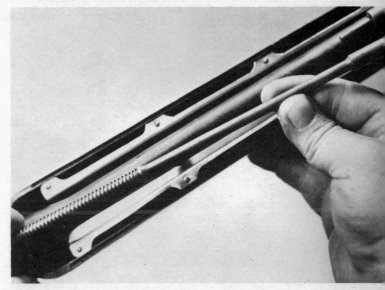

19. Remove the gas piston toward the rear. The gas piston tube can be unscrewed from the rear sight base, but in normal takedown it is best left in place.

20. Drifting out the two cross-pins in the front sight unit will allow the unit to be moved forward. This will release the lower handguard for removal forward and downward. The handguard plate can then be removed toward the rear.

21. The flash hider can be unscrewed from the muzzle by using a wrench of the proper size. The front sight unit can then be taken off toward the front.

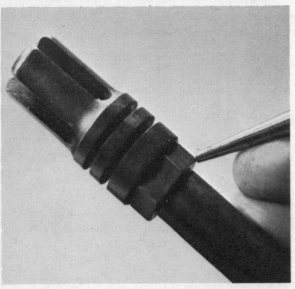

22. The ejection port cover hinge has a grooved tip at the rear for engagement of a tool to nudge it out rearward, releasing the cover and its spring. The hinge pin is often tightly fitted, and unless necessary for repair, it is best left in place. The cover latch plunger and spring are retained by a roll pin.

23. Swing the bolt latch up to the vertical position. Release the safety, restrain the hammer, and pull the trigger, lowering the hammer to the fired position.

24. Remove the C-clip that retains the bolt latch pivot, and push the latch pivot inward for removal.

25. Remove the bolt latch upward. A plunger and spring are retained in the front of the latch by a roll cross-pin. Take out the plug, spring, and plunger downward.

26. Remove the C-clip from the tip of the safety cross-piece on the right side of the frame.

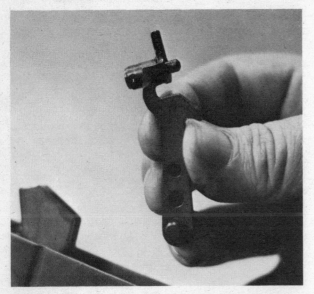

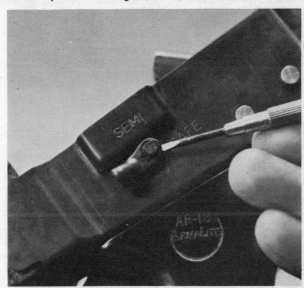

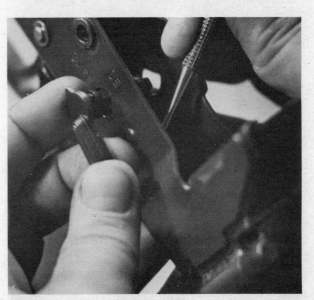

27. Remove the safety indicator lever toward the right. Return the hammer to the cocked position.

28. Insert a tool from the top to engage the hole in the safety spring yoke, and depress the yoke and spring toward the rear. While holding them there, remove the safety toward the left.

29. Slowly release the spring tension, and remove the safety yoke and spring upward.

30. Restrain the hammer, pull the trigger, and lower the hammer to the fired position. Remove the C-clip from the left tip of the hammer pivot, restrain the hammer, and push out the pivot toward the right.

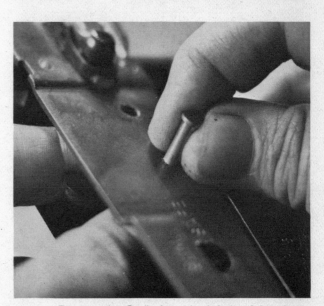

31. Remove the hammer and its spring forward and upward.

32. Remove the C-clip from the left tip of the trigger pivot. Restrain the trigger and sear, and push out the trigger cross-pin toward the right.

33. Remove the trigger assembly upward. Pushing out the pivot sleeve will release the trigger spring for removal, and will also release the secondary sear, or disconnector, for removal. If the sleeve is to be removed, use a large roll-pin punch to avoid deforming it.

34. The magazine catch and its spring are retained by a vertical roll pin which is drifted out upward, and the catch and spring are taken off toward the right.

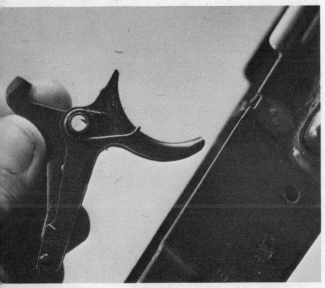

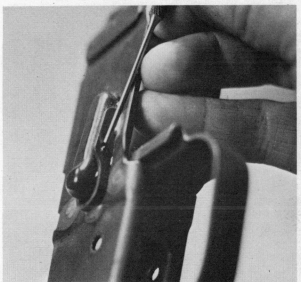

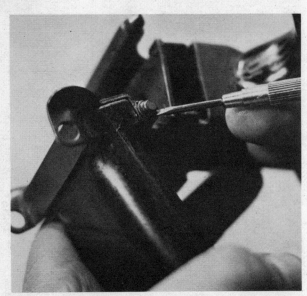

35. The buttstock hinge pin is retained by a C-clip in a groove at its lower tip, and the hinge pin is taken out upward. The buttstock can then be removed.

36. The upper and lower stock latch plungers and their common spring are retained by two roll pins. Drifting out one of the pins will allow removal of one plunger and the spring.

37. The pistol grip is retained by a screw accessible from below, and the grip is taken off downward. The buttstock is retained on its hinge plate by a long screw accessible at the center of the buttplate.

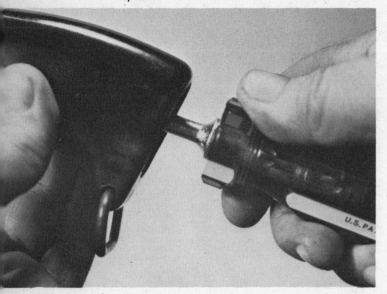

Reassembly Tips:

1. Note that the cam pin hole in the bolt is staked on one side, to prevent the bolt from being reinstalled in the bolt carrier backwards. When replacing the bolt in the carrier, be sure the extractor is on the right.

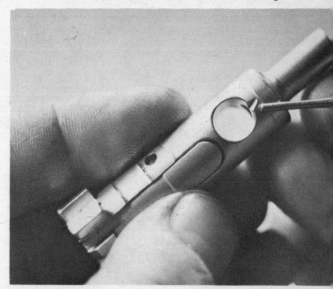

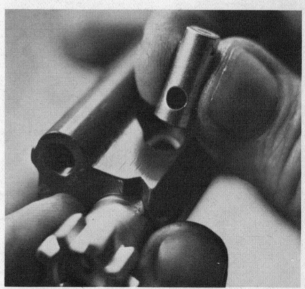

2. When replacing the cam pin, note that the crosshole in the pin must be oriented lengthwise for passage of the firing pin.

COLT AR-15

Data: Colt AR-15
Origin: United States
Manufacturer: Colt Firearms
Hartford, Connecticut
Cartridge: 223 Remington (5.56mm)
Magazine Capacity: 5 and 20 rounds
Over-all length: 38⅜ inches
Barrel length: 20 inches
Weight: 7¼ pounds

While the selective fire M-16 is available to police agencies, many smaller departments and individual officers prefer the semi-auto AR-15. It is also available in a shorter collapsible-stock model with 16-inch barrel. Except for the stock attachment, the two models are mechanically the same, and the instructions will apply to either one.

Disassembly:

1. Remove the magazine, and cycle the action to cock the hammer. Push out the takedown pin, located at the upper rear of the grip frame, toward the right.

2. With the takedown pin stopped in pulled-out position, tip the barrel and receiver assembly upward at the rear.

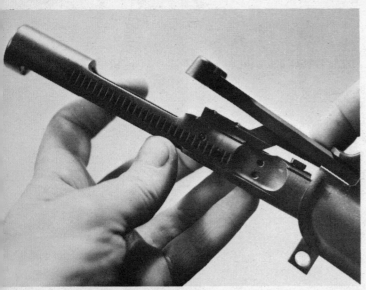

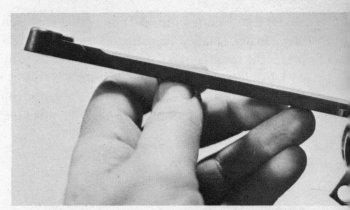

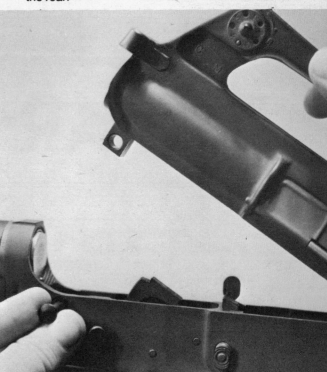

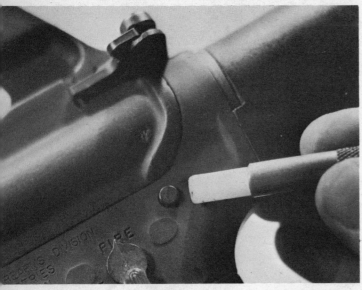

3. Use the charging handle to start the bolt assembly toward the rear, and remove the assembly from the rear of the receiver.

4. Move the charging handle to the rear until it stops, then move it downward and take it out the rear of the receiver.

5. The charging handle latch and its spring are retained in the handle by a vertical roll pin. In normal takedown, it is best left in place.

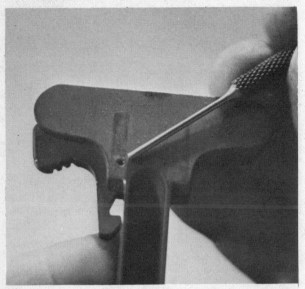

6. Use a small tool to pull out the cotter pin on the left side of the bolt carier, to free the firing pin.

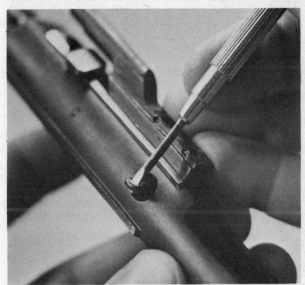

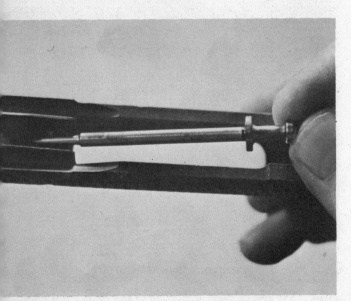

7. Remove the firing pin toward the rear.

8. Rotate the bolt cam pin to clear its flange from beneath the edge of the overhang, and remove the bolt cam pin upward.

9. Remove the bolt from the front of the bolt carrier.

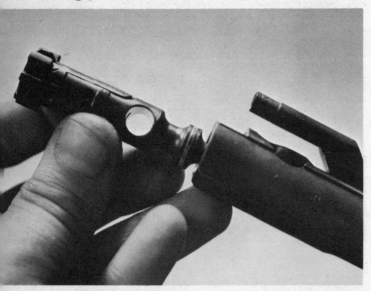

10. The extractor and its coil spring are retained in the bolt by a cross-pin which is easily pushed out in either direction.

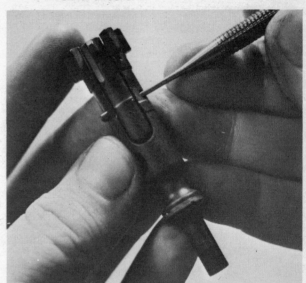

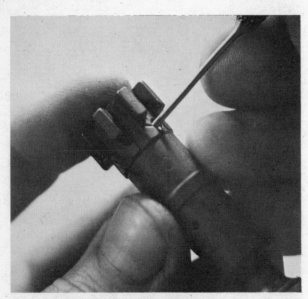

11. The ejector and its spring are also retained by a pin, a small roll pin that crosses the front of the bolt. The ejector spring is quite strong, so restrain the ejector during removal.

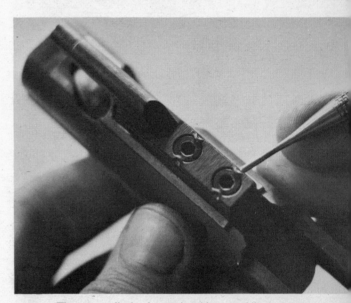

12. The gas cylinder is retained by two Allen screws on top of the bolt carrier, and these are heavily staked in place. *This unit should be removed only if repair or replacement is necessary.*

13. Remove the cap screw at the left end of the receiver pivot. It will be necessary to stabilize the screw-slotted head of the pivot with another large screwdriver on the right side during removal.

14. Use a slim drift punch that will not damage the interior threads to nudge the receiver pivot out toward the right, and separate the barrel and receiver unit from the stock and grip frame assembly.

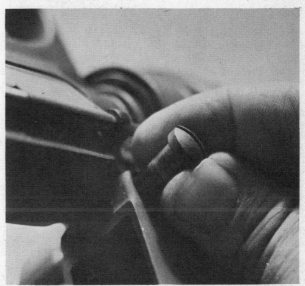

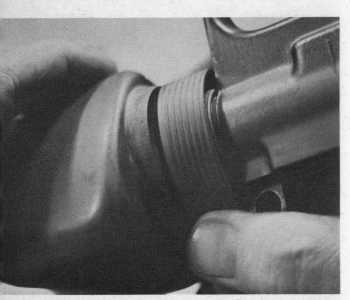

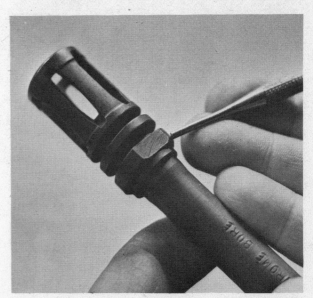

15. Pull back on the grooved slip ring right at the rear of the handguard units, and alternately tip each unit outward at the rear, then remove them rearward.

16. With a wrench of the proper size, unscrew the flash hider from the end of the barrel, and take care not to lose the lock washer behind it.

17. The combination front sight base, gas port unit, and bayonet mount is retained on the barrel by two large cross-pins. When these are drifted out toward the right, the unit can be nudged forward off the barrel. During removal, take care that the gas transfer tube is not damaged.

18. The gas conduit is retained in the sight unit by a roll cross-pin. In normal takedown, this should not be disturbed.

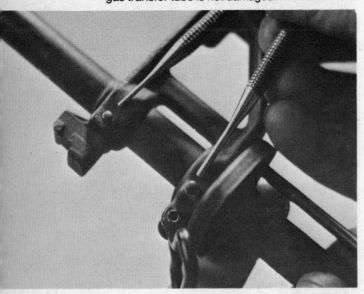

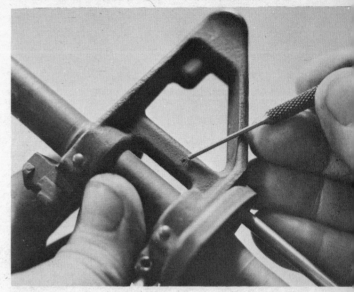

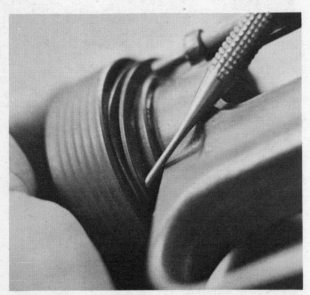

19. Insert a small tool in one of the holes at the top of the large clip-ring at the front of the receiver, and gently pry the ring out of its channel. Moving it rearward will relieve the tension of the circular spring assembly that powers the handguard slip-ring.

20. Move the slip-ring to the rear to give access to the toothed barrel retaining nut, and unscrew the nut counter-clockwise (front view). Take off the retaining nut, slip ring, spring, and clip-ring toward the front.

21. The long pin which forms the hinge for the ejection port cover is retained by a C-clip in a groove near its forward end. Take off the C-clip, and move the hinge pin out toward the rear. **Caution:** *The cover spring will be released as the pin is cleared, so restrain it. Take care that the very small C-clip is not lost.*

22. Restrain the hammer and pull the trigger to lower the hammer to fired position. Push out the hammer pivot pin toward either side, controlling the hammer against its spring tension.

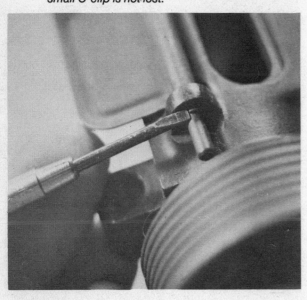

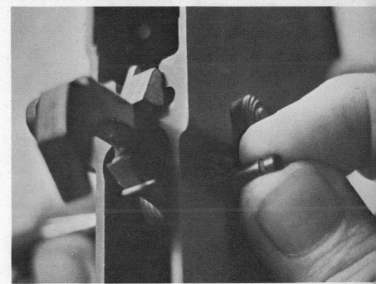

23. Remove the hammer and its spring upward. The spring is easily detached from the hammer.

24. Push the trigger pin just far enough toward the right that the disconnector is cleared, and remove the disconnector from the top of the grip frame.

25. Set the safety halfway between its two positions, and use a nylon drift punch on the right side to nudge it toward the left, then remove it.

26. Remove the trigger pin, and take out the trigger assembly upward. The trigger spring and disconnector spring are easily detached from the trigger.

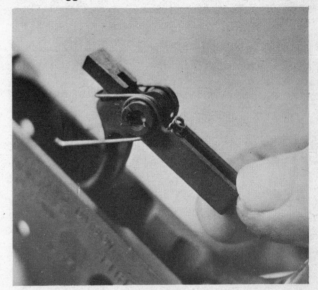

27. The magazine catch is removed by pushing it toward the left beyond its normal magazine release point, then unscrewing the catch piece from the button. The button and spring are then taken off toward the right, and the catch piece toward the left. The catch piece is unscrewed counterclockwise, left-side view.

28. The hold-open device and its spring are retained on the left side of the grip frame by a roll pin, and after removal of the pin they are taken off toward the left.

29. Restrain the recoil buffer against the tension of the recoil spring, and depress the buffer stop plunger. **Caution:** *The spring is strong, so take care to keep it under control.*

30. Slowly release the tension of the spring, and remove the buffer and spring toward the front.

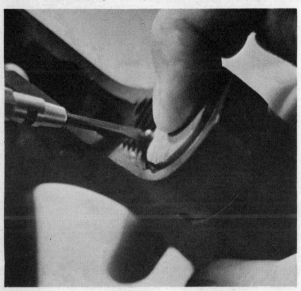

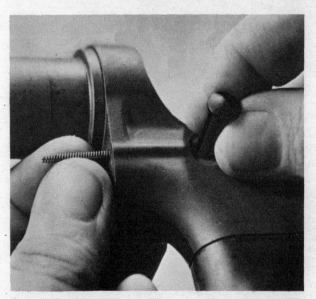

31. Remove the upper screw in the buttplate and remove the buttstock toward the rear. Take care not to lose the takedown pin retaining plunger and its spring at the rear of the grip frame. Removal of the lower screw in the buttplate will give access to the mechanism of the storage compartment cover and its latch.

32. Remove the takedown pin spring and plunger from the rear of the grip frame. The takedown pin can then be removed toward the right.

33. The pistol grip is removed by backing out a screw accessible through the bottom of the grip. Note that this will also release the safety plunger and its spring for removal downward.

34. The lower section of the trigger guard is retained at the rear by a roll cross-pin. After this is removed, the section can be swung downward, and a very small roll pin in its forward hinge will be exposed for removal. The hinge pin can then be taken out toward the right, and the lower section removed.

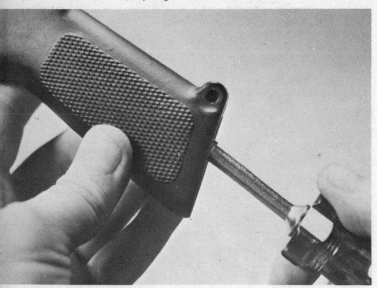

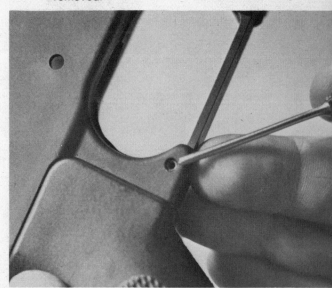

Reassembly Tips:

1. When replacing the safety lever, use a tool on the right side to depress the safety plunger as the safety is pushed into place.

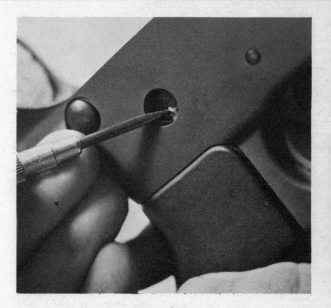

2. When replacing the cocking handle, remember that its forward end must be inserted into the receiver and then moved upward into its track.

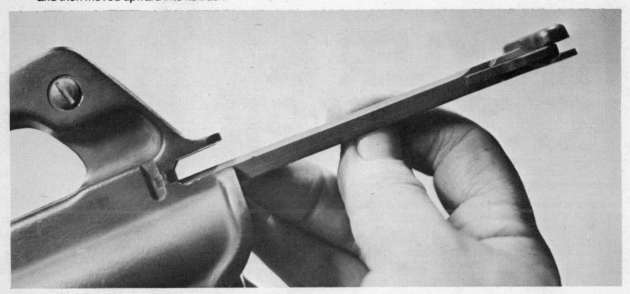

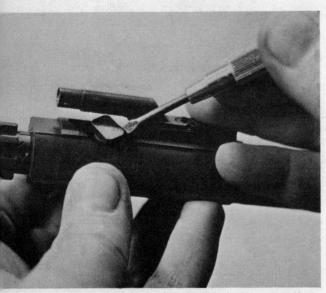

3. When replacing the bolt in the bolt carrier, note that the extractor must be oriented to the upper right, and the ejector to the lower left. Also, remember to turn the bolt cam pin so its flange is beneath the edge of the gas cylinder.

HECKLER & KOCH HK 91

Data: Heckler & Koch HK 91
Origin: West Germany
Manufacturer: Heckler & Koch GmbH
Oberndorf/Neckar
Cartridge: 308 Winchester (7.62x 51mm)
Magazine Capacity: 5 and 20 rounds
Over-all length: 40¼ inches
Barrel length: 19 inches
Weight: 10.3 pounds

The HK 91 is the semi-auto version of the selective-fire G3, the standard West German military rifle. Except for the full-auto system, the two guns are mechanically very similar, and most of the instructions will apply. There is also a version in 223 caliber, the HK 33, and all three guns are available in retractable-stock models.

Disassembly:

1. Remove the magazine, and cycle the action to cock the internal hammer. Push out the two locking cross-pins at the lower rear of the receiver. Cross-holes are provided in the buttstock for storage of the pins during disassembly.

2. Remove the buttstock and back plate assembly toward the rear. The recoil spring and its guide and the buffer assembly can be taken out of the stock, if necessary, by removal of two slotted screws inside the front of the buttstock. Control the springs during this operation.

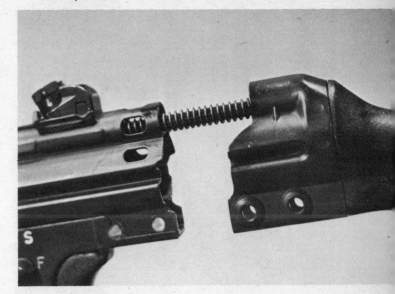

3. Tip the grip frame down at the rear, and remove it downward.

4. Turn the safety lever up to vertical position, and remove it toward the left. The hammer should be in the fired position for this operation.

5. Remove the sub-frame from the pistol-grip unit. If it is very tight, it may be necessary to pry it gently at the front to start it.

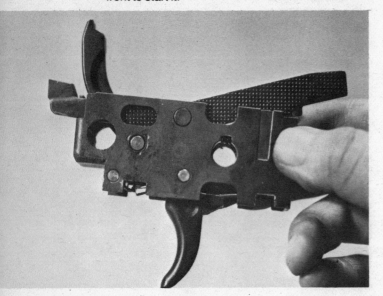

6. Restrain the ejector, and push the ejector pivot out toward the left.

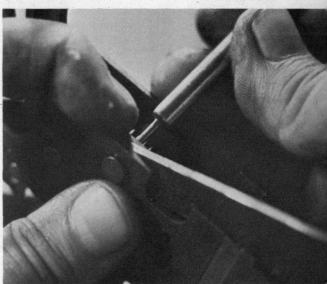

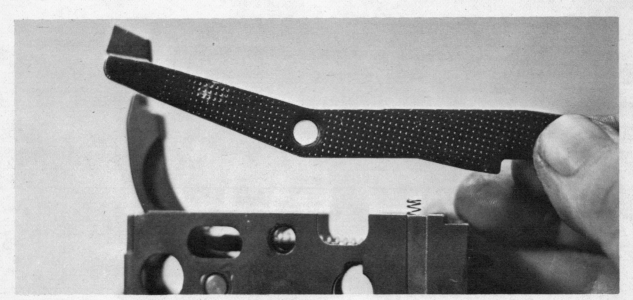

7. Remove the ejector upward, and take out its vertical spring at the rear.

8. Restrain the hammer spring and its guide at the top, and insert a tool through the side opening to lift the forward end of the guide out of its engagement with the hammer.

9. Remove the hammer spring and guide upward and toward the front.

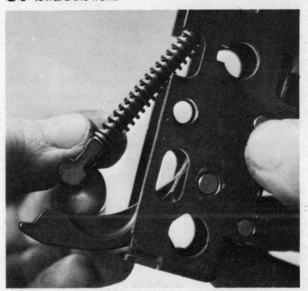

10. Remove the hammer pivot toward either side.

11. Remove the hammer upward.

12. Restrain the sear spring and its roller at the front, and push out the sear cross-pin toward either side.

13. Remove the sear spring and its roller, or mounting sleeve, downward.

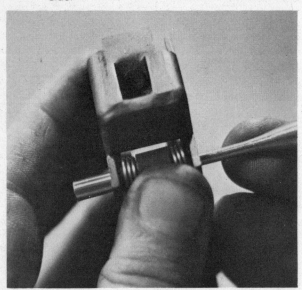

14. Unhook the trigger spring from its shelf on the trigger, on the left side at the rear, and move the spring arm downward and forward, relieving its tension. **Caution:** *Keep fingertips clear, as the released spring can cause injury.*

15. Push out the trigger pivot pin toward either side.

16. Remove the trigger assembly downward. The sear is easily lifted out from the trigger top, and the trigger spring from the left side of the trigger.

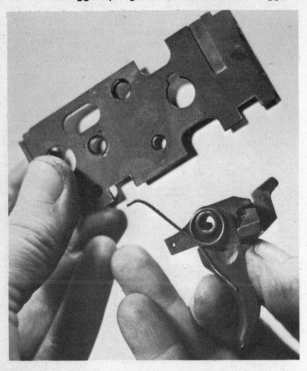

17. A roll pin at the front of the sear retains an internal plunger and spring. If this is to be removed, control the plunger and spring, and ease them out.

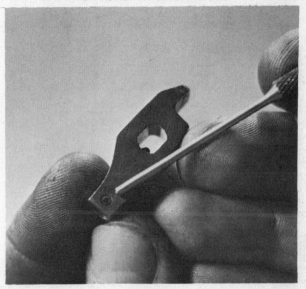

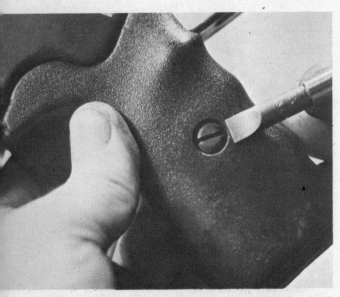

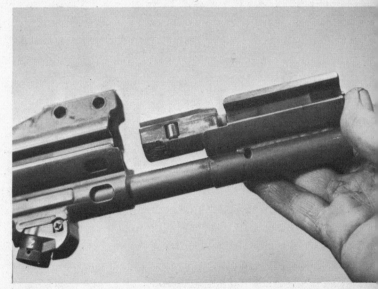

18. A single screw on the right side retains the pistol-grip handle on the grip frame. After the screw is removed, the handle is taken off downward.

19. Remove the bolt assembly from the rear of the receiver.

20. Turn the bolt head 90 degrees toward the right, and remove the bolt head toward the front.

21. Insert a small screwdriver in the loop of the extractor spring on the bolt head, and lift it just enough to clear its shoulder on the extractor, then pull the spring out toward the front.

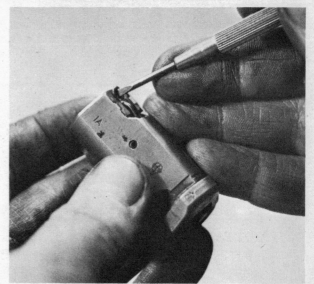

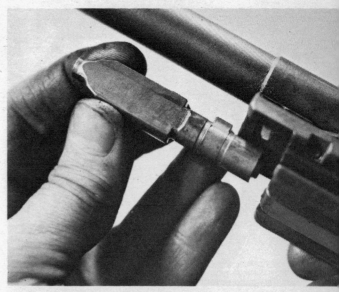

22. After removal of the spring, the extractor can be lifted out of its recess in the bolt head. The locking rollers are retained by an inner bracket which is held by a roll pin. The pin can be drifted down into the bolt head, and the bracket and rollers moved out toward the side. In normal takedown, this unit is best left in place.

23. Rotate the locking piece one-half turn in either direction, and remove it toward the front.

24. Remove the firing pin toward the front, along with its spring.

25. The bolt head locking lever and its spring are retained on the bolt carrier by a cross-pin. If these parts are to be removed, keep them under control, as the spring is very strong.

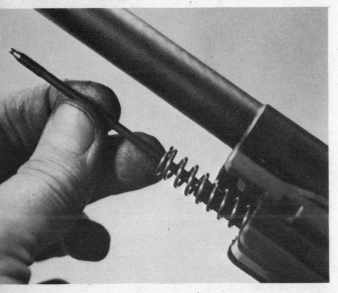

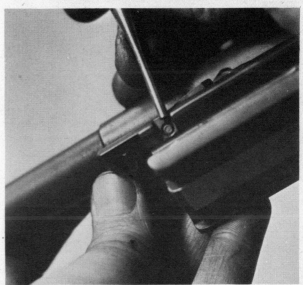

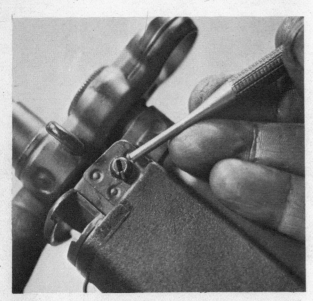

26. Push out the locking pin at the front of the handguard.

27. Tip the handguard down at the front, then remove it toward the front and downward

28. It is possible to remove the cocking handle assembly by aligning its cross-pin with the access holes in the sleeve and drifting out the pin. The handle and spring are then removed outward, and the internal rod is moved out toward the rear. In normal takedown, this unit is best left in place.

29. The magazine catch button is retained on the cross-piece by a vertical roll pin. When the pin is drifted out, the button and spring are released toward the right, and the catch piece is taken off toward the left.

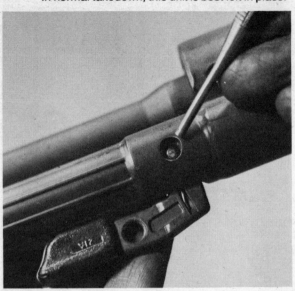

30. The gas piston cap at the front is retained by a plunger and spring. Depress the plunger, and take off the cap toward the front.

31. Engage a tool or a piece of bar stock with the opposed notches in the front of the flash hider, and unscrew it from the end of the barrel. Take care not to lose the retaining spring.

32. The rear sight is both horizontally adjusted and retained by a large Phillips screw on top. If this is removed, take care that the lock washer and the flat spring plate are not lost. The turret locking ball and spring will also be released on the underside of the sight, so keep these small parts under control. Unless repair is necessary, the sight should be left in place.

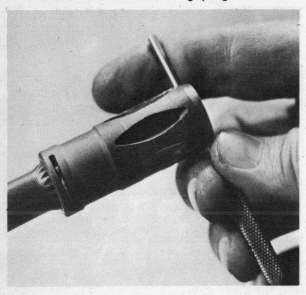

Reassembly Tips:

1. When replacing the bolt head in the carrier, it will be necessary to depress the rear of the locking lever or lift its front beak to engage with its track on the bolt head.

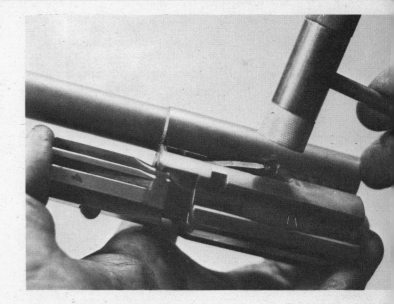

2. When reassembling the trigger group, install the sear spring assembly first, being sure that its upper arms are in front of the hammer pivot projections inside. Lift the lower portion of the spring, and insert one of the major retaining pins, as shown, to hold the spring during installation of the sear and trigger assembly. When the parts are installed, remove the pin, and be sure the small roller at the rear tip of the spring engages the underside of the sear.

3. Before replacing the bolt and bolt carrier in the receiver, the bolt head must be moved forward slightly in the carrier, as shown, to retract the locking rollers.

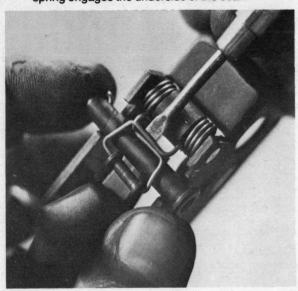

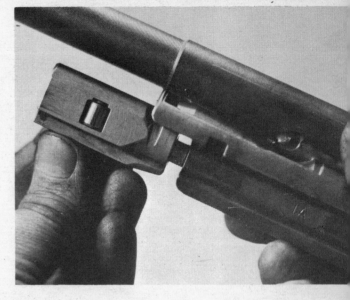

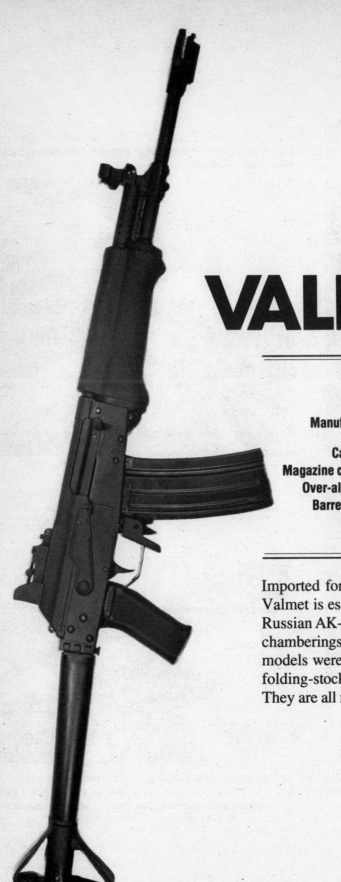

VALMET 76FS

Data:	Valmet 76 FS
Origin:	Finland
Manufacturer:	Valmet Oy
	Helsinki
Cartridge:	223 Rem. (5.56mm)
Magazine capacity:	15 and 30 rounds
Over-all length:	36⅝ inches
Barrel length:	16⅝ inches
Weight:	8¾ pounds

Imported for a time by Interarms in several models, the Valmet is essentially a modified semi-auto version of the Russian AK-series of guns. The Valmet was offered in two chamberings, the 223 and the 7.62x 39mm, and the models were the 62/S, 62/FS, 71/S, and 76/FS. The last folding-stock model, the M76/FS, is the gun shown here. They are all mechanically similar, but not identical.

Disassembly:

1. Remove the magazine, and cycle the action to cock the internal hammer. Set the safety in the off-safe position. Depress the receiver cover latch, and lift the rear of the cover upward.

2. Detach the receiver cover and remove it upward and toward the rear.

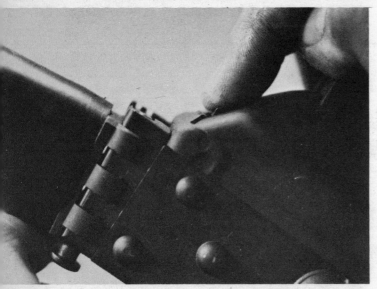

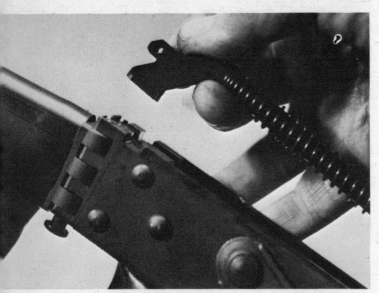

3. Move the rear base of the recoil spring guide forward to detach it from its seat in the receiver, lift it upward, and remove the guide and spring toward the rear.

4. Move the bolt carrier assembly toward the rear until the piston is clear of its sleeve at the front. Lift the rear of the carrier as it is moved toward the rear, and remove the assembly.

5. Move the bolt rearward in the carrier until it stops, turn it to the left (counter-clockwise, front view) until its lug clears, then remove the bolt toward the front.

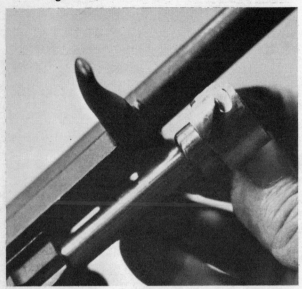

6. If the gas piston is damaged and requires replacement, drifting out this roll pin will release it for removal toward the front. Otherwise, don't disturb it.

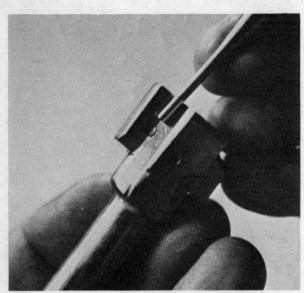

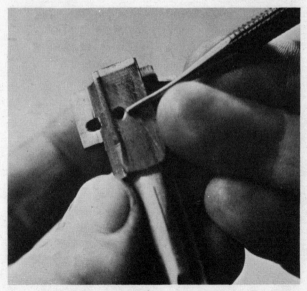

7. The extractor and its spring are retained by the larger of the two pins which cross the front of the bolt. The pin is drifted out toward the right. Restrain the extractor and spring, and ease them out.

8. The smaller of the two pins in the bolt retains the firing pin and its spring. Restrain the firing pin at the rear, drift out the pin upward, and remove the firing pin and spring toward the rear.

9. Move the gas tube toward the rear, lift it slightly to clear its lower edges, and remove it rearward.

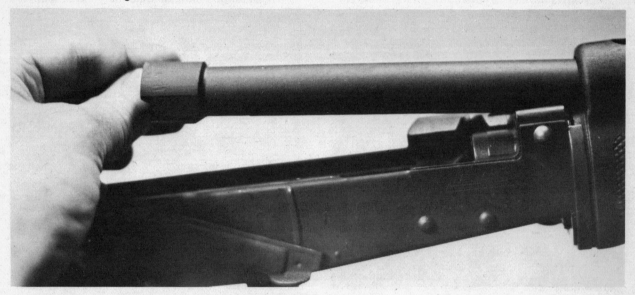

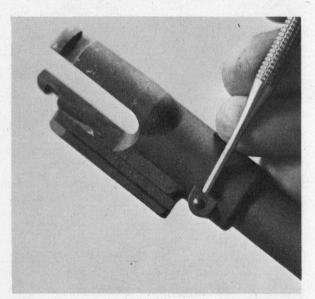

10. The flash hider is retained on the end of the barrel by a cross-pin which is driven out toward the right.

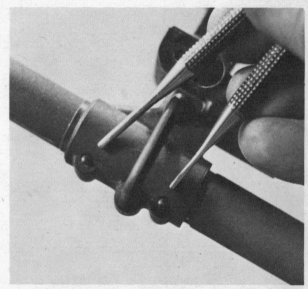

11. The combination front sight base and gas port unit is retained by two cross-pins. After the pins are drifted out toward the right, the unit can be nudged forward off the barrel.

12. The handguard is retained by a threaded nut-plate at the front, and the plate has spanner-holes for the use of a special wrench. In the absence of this tool, use a nylon drift punch set in one of the holes to free the nut, then unscrew it, counter-clockwise (front view). Take off the nut-plate, washer, and the second nut, then remove the handguard toward the front. The rear handguard plate will also be freed for removal. The barrel and the bolt cam plate are cross-pinned and riveted in place, and routine removal is neither practical nor advisable. The ejector is also riveted in place on the left inner wall of the receiver, and it should not be disturbed unless necessary for repair.

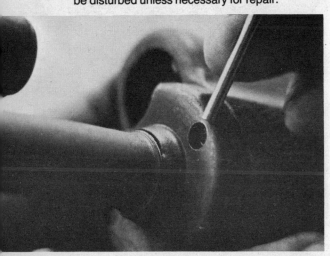

13. Restrain the hammer, pull the trigger, and ease the hammer over past its normal forward position. Insert a tool inside the receiver to lift the front loop of the hammer pin retaining spring, and push the hammer pin out toward the left. Move the safety upward to clear the pin.

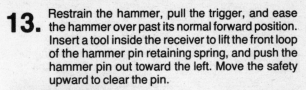

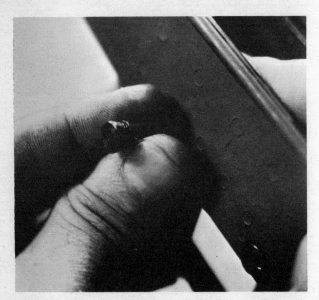

14. Restrain the hammer, and remove the hammer pin toward the left.

15. Insert a tool to unhook the rear tips of the hammer spring from the trigger, and move the hammer and its attached spring forward. Turn the hammer assembly to clear it, and remove the hammer and spring from the bottom of the receiver.

16. Insert a tool to slide the pin retaining spring forward, and remove it from the bottom of the receiver.

17. Push out the trigger pin and remove it toward the left. Restrain the sear while this is done.

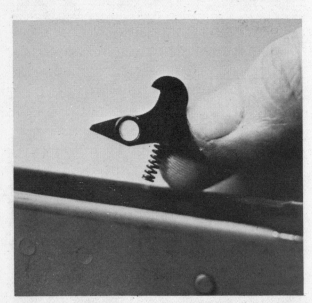

18. Remove the sear and its coil spring from the top of the receiver.

19. Remove the trigger from the top of the receiver.

20. Turn the safety lever up to the vertical position, move it toward the left, then slightly toward the rear. Remove the lever toward the right.

21. The magazine catch and its torsion spring are retained by a riveted cross-pin, and these parts should be removed only for repair. The pistol grip piece is retained by a screw and lock-washer inside the receiver.

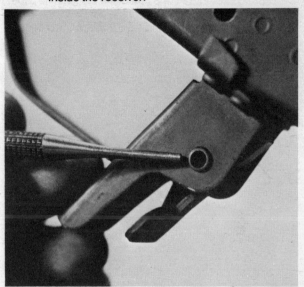

22. The folding buttstock is retained by a vertical hinge pin. After the pin is driven out downward, the stock latch spring can be slid toward the left, releasing the stock latch for removal downward.

23. The latch that holds the stock in folded position is retained on the back of the rear handguard plate by a hexagonal nut, and can be removed with a small wrench of the proper size.

246 : Valmet 76/FS

Reassembly Tips:

1. When reassembling the internal components of the receiver, be sure to install the safety lever first, as this cannot be done with the sear and trigger assembly in place. Install the sear and trigger next, then the lock spring, being sure the rear tip of the spring is below the trigger pin. Install the hammer, lift the lock spring, and insert the hammer pin beneath the spring. Finally, hook the rear tips of the hammer spring back into the top rear of the trigger. The photo shows the interior of the receiver, with the parts properly installed, and the hammer in cocked position.

2. When replacing the bolt carrier assembly, position the rear of the carrier over the rear of the receiver as shown, then move it downward to engage its tracks with the flanges inside the receiver.

SECTION VI

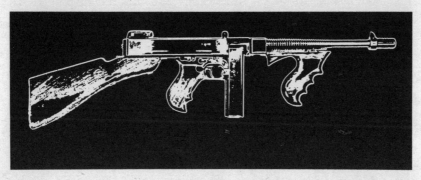

The guns with full-auto capability are invariably reserved for special situations or special teams. The U.S. Secret Service, for example is partial to the Israeli Uzi. Many police departments, even the smaller ones, have a venerable Thompson or an ex-military Reising in the arms locker, for use only in extraordinary emergencies. These guns are usually available to a very limited number of personnel, as proper firing techniques require special training. The police shotgun is better for crowd control, but *only if it has to be fired*. The very presence of a submachine gun will often quiet the most unruly mob, without the necessity of firing a single shot.

INGRAM MODEL 10

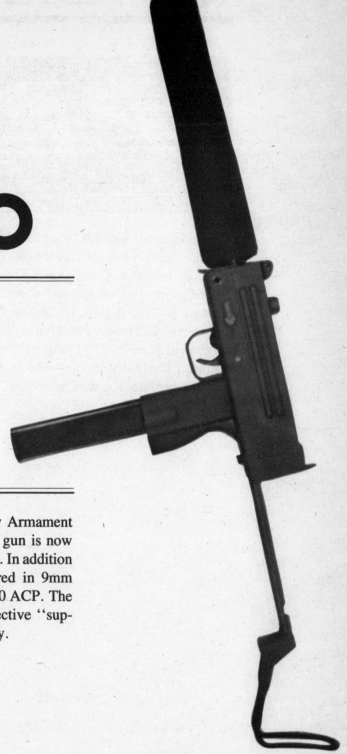

Data:	Ingram Model 10
Origin:	United States
Manufacturer:	RPB Industries, Inc. Atlanta, Georgia
Cartridge:	45 ACP
Magazine capacity:	30 rounds
Over-all length:	31¾ inches (with silencer, stock extended)
Barrel length:	5¾ inches
Weight:	6¼ pounds

Originally made as the MAC-10 by Military Armament Corporation, this neat, flat little submachine gun is now called the Ingram Model 10 by RPB Industries. In addition to the 45 ACP chambering, it is also offered in 9mm Luger. A smaller gun, the Model 11, is in 380 ACP. The guns are mechanically the same. A very effective ''suppressor'' (silencer) is available as an accessory.

Disassembly:

1. Remove the magazine, and leave the bolt in the forward position. Unscrew the suppressor, and remove it from the barrel.

2. Push out the takedown pin, located at the lower front of the receiver, toward the right.

3. Lift the front of the receiver assembly, move the assembly forward, and detach it from the grip frame.

4. Move the bolt assembly to the rear of the receiver, and align the bolt handle with the larger opening at the rear of its track. Pull the bolt handle out upward. If it is very tight, insert a drift punch from below and nudge it out.

5. Remove the bolt assembly toward the rear.

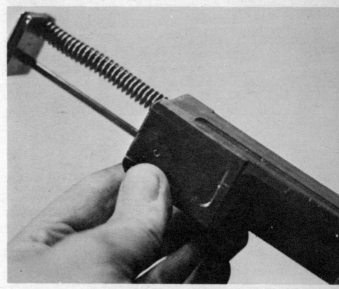

6. The barrel is threaded into the receiver and also retained by a large roll cross-pin. Routine removal is not recommended.

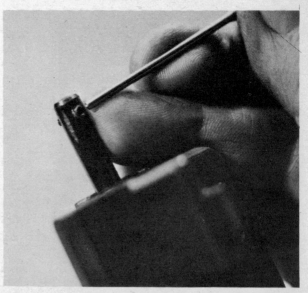

7. The recoil spring assembly is retained in the bolt by a roll cross-pin at the front of the recoil spring guide. Compress the recoil spring slightly to push the guide out the front of the bolt, drift out the cross-pin, and the spring and guide assembly can be removed toward the rear. **Caution:** *When the pin is out, control the compressed spring.*

8. The extractor is retained by a roll cross-pin which is drifted out toward the right.

9. After the pin is removed, insert a drift punch from the rear, and nudge the extractor out toward the front.

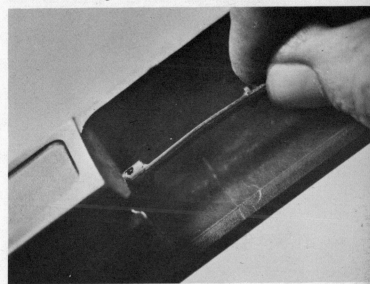

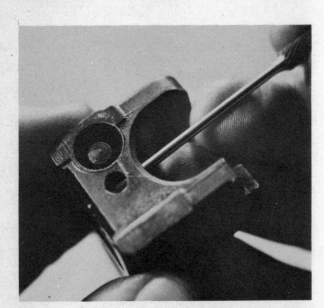

10. The bolt handle retaining plunger and its spring are retained at the front of the bolt by a vertical roll pin which is drifted out upward. Restrain the spring as the pin is removed, and take out the spring and plunger toward the front.

11. Lift the front L-shaped tip of the selector positioning spring slightly, and push the selector crosspiece toward the left.

12. Restrain the sear, and remove the selector toward the left.

13. Remove the sear and its spring from the top of the receiver.

14. Remove the disconnector from the top of the receiver.

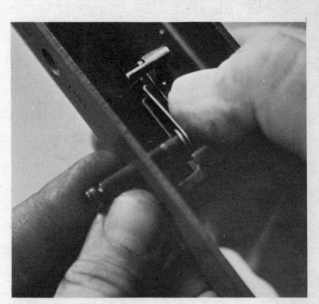

15. Restrain the trigger, and push out the trigger pin toward the left.

16. Remove the trigger assembly upward.

17. The spring is easily detached from the trigger. The sear trip is retained on the front of the trigger by a roll cross-pin, and can be removed if necessary.

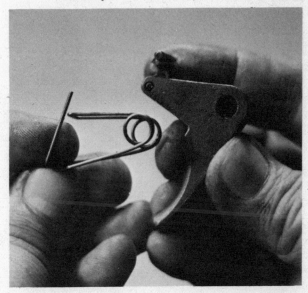

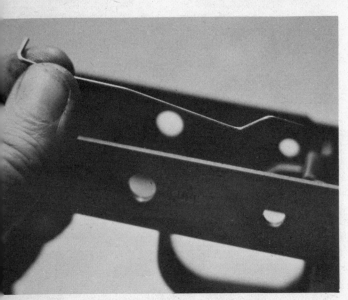

18. Remove the pivot pin locking spring.

19. The safety assembly is retained by a roll cross-pin in the safety button. After the pin is drifted out, the button is taken off downward, and the safety block, spring, and plunger upward.

20. Remove the screw at the center of the backstrap piece on the pistol grip.

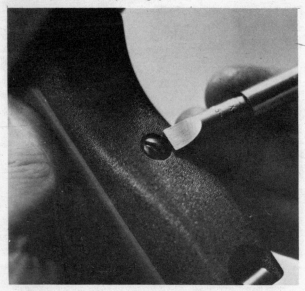

21. Move the backstrap piece toward the rear for removal. Note that the magazine catch spring bears on the backstrap, so remove it slowly.

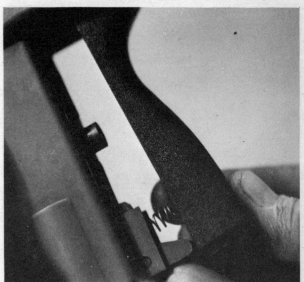

22. Push out the cross-pin at the lower rear of the grip frame, and remove the magazine catch and its spring.

23. Depress and hold the stock latch button, and remove the stock toward the rear. The stock shoulder piece is retained by a C-clip on its hinge pin.

24. Inside the frame at the rear, depress the stock latch cross-pin slightly, and move the pin out toward either side.

25. After the cross-pin is removed, the stock latch and its plunger and spring can be taken out upward.

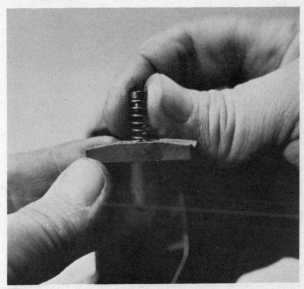

Reassembly Tips:

1. When replacing the trigger assembly, turn the sear trip in at the front to bear against the lower arm of the trigger spring, and use it to keep the spring to the rear while the cross-pin is inserted.

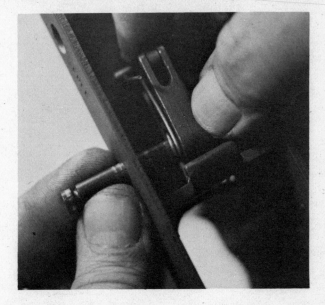

2. This top view of the grip frame shows the parts installed in proper order.

3. When replacing the extractor, note that it must be oriented so the hole in the extractor base will align with the cross-hole in the bolt. When the extractor is in position, insert a tapered drift punch to check this alignment before installing the cross-pin.

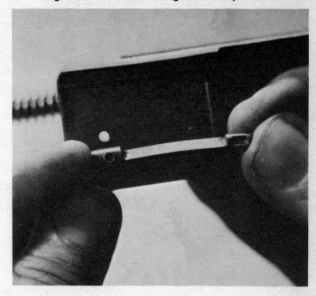

REISING MODEL 50

Data: Reising Model 50
Origin: United States
Manufacturer: Harrington & Richardson
Worcester, Massachusetts
Cartridge: 45 ACP
Magazine capacity: 12 and 20 rounds
Over-all length: 35¾ inches
Barrel length: 11 inches
Weight: 6¾ pounds

Designed by Eugene G. Reising, the Model 50 was made by Harrington & Richardson from 1940 through World War II, with a total production of about 100,000 guns. The Model 50 and a folding-stock version, the Model 55, were produced mainly for the U.S. Marines and the British Purchasing Commission. After the war, many of these guns were released to local law enforcement agencies in the United States.

Disassembly:

1. Remove the magazine, and set the fire selector in the full-auto position. Pull the trigger to drop the hammer to the fired position. Unscrew the takedown knob, located on the underside just behind the magazine housing. If the knob is tight, there is a slot for a coin or a large screwdriver. Lift the action out of the stock.

2. Unscrew the large endcap at the rear of the receiver, controlling it against the pressure of the hammer spring.

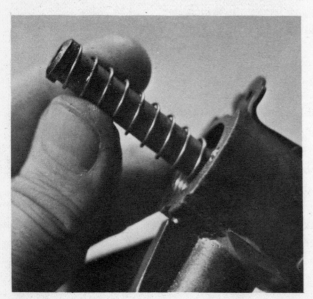

3. Remove the hammer spring toward the rear.

4. Tilt the action, pull the trigger, and remove the hammer from the rear of the receiver.

5. Drift out the front and rear magazine housing retainers toward the left.

6. Remove the magazine housing downward.

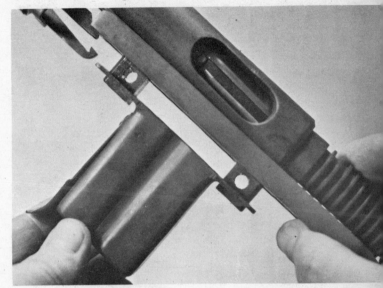

7. The magazine catch, which is its own spring, is retained on the back of the magazine housing by a single screw.

8. Move the action slide toward the rear until a hole is visible in the bolt spring guide. Insert a pin or tool in the hole and ease the slide forward, capturing the spring.

9. Move the slide assembly forward until it is stopped by the rear magazine housing mount, and move the front of the disconnector and connector away from the receiver for clearance. Tilt the front of the action slide away from the barrel.

10. Move the rear of the action slide outward, and twist it toward either side to clear the bolt contact lug from the receiver. Remove the slide assembly from the receiver. Restrain the bolt spring guide at the rear, remove the pin or tool, and remove the spring and guide toward the rear.

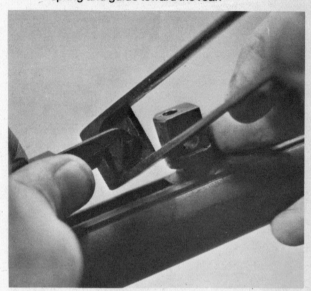

11. Tilt the action upward, pull the trigger, and remove the bolt from the rear of the receiver.

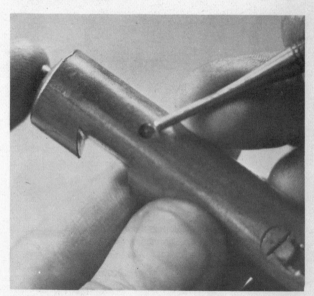

12. The firing pin and its return spring are retained in the bolt by a cross-pin which is drifted out toward the left. Restrain the firing pin as this is removed.

13. The extractor is retained on the right side of the bolt by a screw. After the screw is removed, insert a tool to gently pry the extractor from its recess.

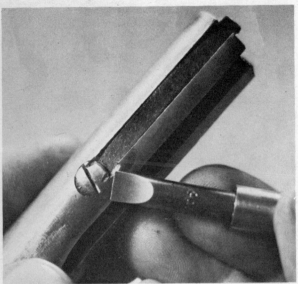

14. Remove the two screws that retain the selector and its positioning spring, and remove these parts toward the right.

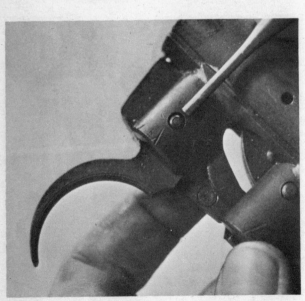

15. Push out the cross-pin that retains the trigger and disconnector.

16. Remove the trigger and disconnector assembly downward. The trigger and disconnector can be separated by drifting out their link pin. The trigger spring and plunger, and the disconnector spring, can now be removed.

18. Remove the sear and connector assembly downward. The spring is easily removed from the top of the sear, and the connector and its spring and plunger can now be removed.

17. Push out the sear cross-pin.

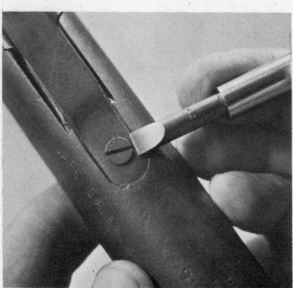

19. The rear sight is retained by a single screw.

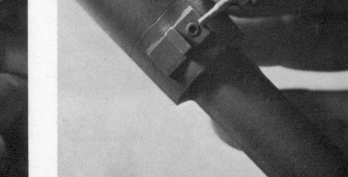

20. The front sight is retained in its dove-tail by a vertical Allen screw.

Reassembly Tips:

1. Here are right and left side views of the trigger, sear, disconnector, and connector assembly in proper order.

When replacing the action slide, be sure its upper rear lug engages the recess on the underside of the bolt.

SMITH & WESSON M76

Data:	Smith & Wesson Model 76
Origin:	United States
Manufacturer:	Smith & Wesson Springfield, Massachusetts
Cartridge:	9mm Luger
Magazine capacity:	36 rounds
Over-all length:	30½ inches (stock extended)
Barrel length:	8 inches
Weight:	7¼ pounds

The S&W M76 was an excellent design which came along at the wrong time. Introduced in 1967, the gun was intended for both military and police use, but no military contracts developed. Most of the few thousand guns made were sold to law enforcement agencies, and the M76 was discontinued by 1970. Many are still in use, and the gun also has considerable collector value.

Disassembly:

1. With the bolt in the forward position and the magazine removed, depress the barrel collar detent toward the rear, and unscrew the collar and cooling jacket for removal toward the front.

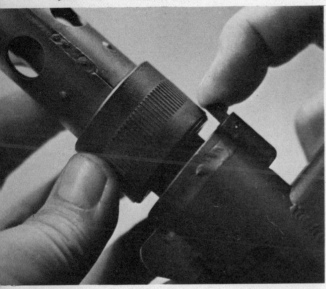

2. Remove the barrel toward the front.

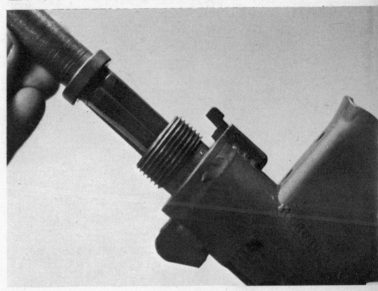

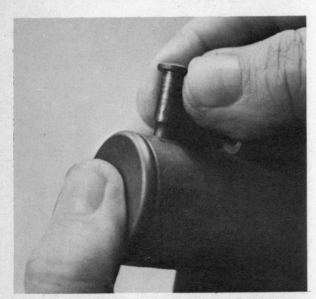

3. Fold the buttstock, restrain the receiver endcap, and push out the retaining pin upward. **Caution:** *Even with the bolt forward, the recoil spring has considerable tension, so keep the endpiece under control.*

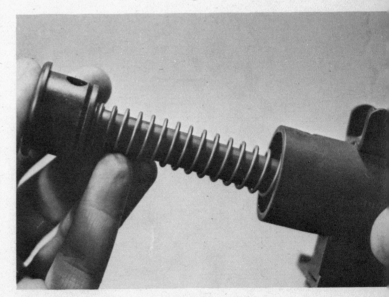

4. When the pin is out, slowly release the spring tension, and remove the endcap, guide, and spring toward the rear.

5. Move the bolt back until the bolt handle aligns with the larger opening at the end of its track, and remove the bolt handle toward the right.

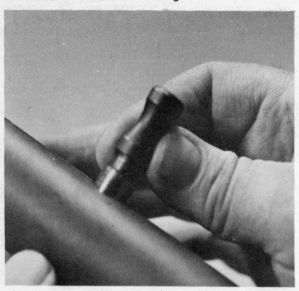

6. Remove the bolt toward the rear.

7. The extractor is retained by a roll cross-pin at the front of the bolt. The pin can be drifted out toward either side.

8. Remove the extractor upward, and take out the extractor spring from its recess.

10. Flex the lower arm of the stock and its plate away from the bottom of the grip piece, and remove the pistol grip toward the rear and downward.

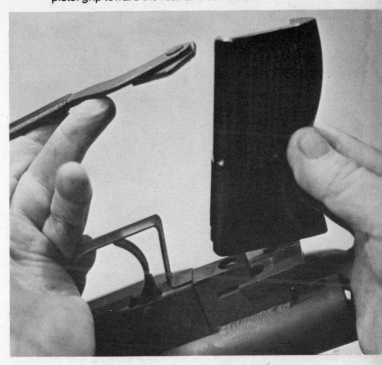

9. With a coin or a large screwdriver, unscrew the large bolt at the bottom of the pistol grip.

11. Unfold the stock to the rear, and tip the trigger sub-frame down at the rear. Remove the trigger sub-frame downward and toward the rear.

12. Remove the C-clip from the left tip of the sear pivot, and push out the sear pivot toward the right.

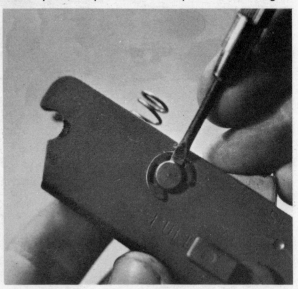

13. Remove the sear and its attached spring upward. The spring is easily removed from its post.

14. The selector (and its twin levers, balls, and springs) is heavily staked at the end of its cross-shaft on each side. Removal is not feasible in normal takedown.

15. The trigger cross-pin is roll-riveted on the left side, and this system is not removed in normal takedown. The forward trigger guard rivet also retains two leaf springs inside the frame, the springs powering the trigger and trigger bar. All of these parts should be removed only for repair purposes, and a new rivet and trigger pin will probably be needed for reassembly. The trigger bar can be separated from the trigger by drifting out the connecting cross-pin.

16. Removal of the pistol grip bolt will have freed the buttstock base plates, and the buttstock can be removed toward the rear. The lower stock plate is retained by a riveted hinge-post. The upper mount hinge is also riveted over a washer at the top, retaining the mount and lock spring. Removal should be only for repair.

17. The ejector is spot-welded in place, and is not routinely removed. To replace a broken ejector, the spot-welds must be ground away, and the ejector is then driven out toward the left. The sights and sling loops are also welded in place.

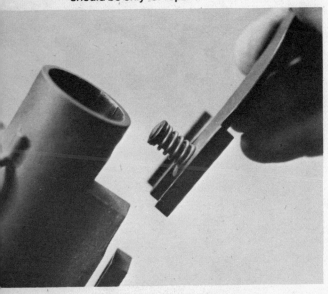

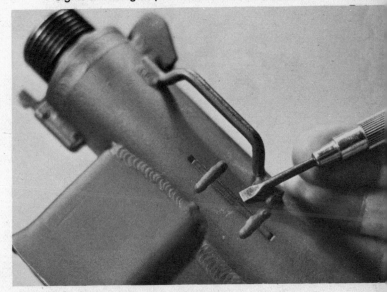

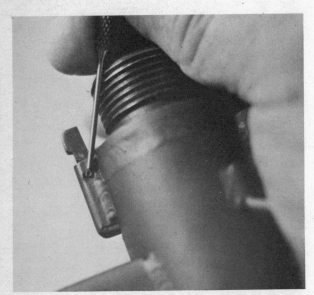

18. The barrel collar detent and its spring are retained by a small roll pin. The detent and its spring are removed toward the front.

19. The magazine catch and its spring are retained by a cross-pin that is roll-riveted on the left side, and this system should be removed only for repair. If removal is necessary, use a drift punch small enough to enter the hollow end on the left, and drift the pin out toward the right. For replacement, a new pin may be necessary.

Reassembly Tips:

1. When replacing the trigger sub-frame, it is necessary to pull the magazine catch downward and hold it out of the way as the sub-frame is moved into place.

THOMPSON MODEL 1921

Data: Thompson Model 1921
Origin: United States
Manufacturer: Colt Firearms
Hartford, Connecticut
Cartridge: 45 ACP
Magazine capacity: 20, 30, and 50 rounds
Over-all length: 33¾ inches
Barrel length: 10½ inches
Weight: 10¾ pounds

Apparently, quite a number of venerable Thompson guns are still in use with many departments around the country. In my own area, both the local police and the sheriff's department have a Thompson in the arms locker. Mechanically, there is very little difference between the Model 1921 and Model 1928, and most parts will interchange. The Model 1921 gun shown here has a Model 1928 recoil spring assembly.

Disassembly:

1. Remove the magazine, depress the stock release button, and slide the buttstock off toward the rear.

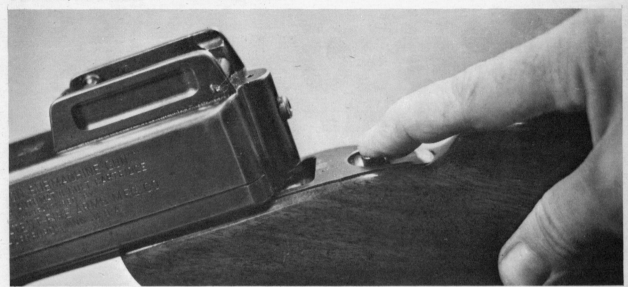

2. With the bolt in the forward position, set the safety to "fire" and the selector to "full auto." Pull the trigger and hold it to the rear. Depress the frame latch button on the underside at the rear.

3. Keeping the trigger pulled to the rear, move the grip frame off toward the rear.

4. Fold a small piece of leather around the blade tip of a large screwdriver (to avoid marring the frame), and insert the tip on the right side between the upper part of the pivot plate and its short middle spring-arm. Turn the screwdriver to lever the arm downward, and push the rocker pivot pin toward the left.

5. Repeat this operation with the longer lower arm of the pivot plate, levering the spring arm clear of the notch in the safety shaft, and moving the safety toward the left.

6. Remove the safety toward the left.

7. Remove the selector lever, which is also the rocker pivot, toward the left.

8. Remove the rocker piece upward.

9. The pivot plate is now removed toward the right. If the plate is tight, use a non-marring punch to nudge its two cross-shafts, the sear and trigger pivots, but do this alternately and equally to avoid deforming the plate. Take care to exert no pressure on the spring arms during removal. When the plate is free enough to be grasped and pulled out toward the right, restrain the sear and trigger assemblies, as they will be released.

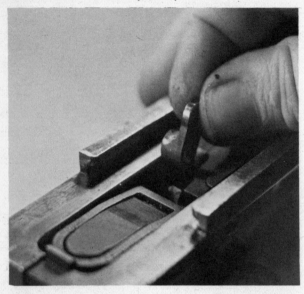

10. Remove the sear assembly upward. The sear, sear lever, and their attendant springs are easily separated after removal.

11. Remove the trigger assembly upward. The trip is easily lifted off the top of the trigger, and the spring can be taken out of its well at the front.

12. The disconnector is taken off the trigger toward the left, and its spring removed from its well in the trigger.

13. Move the magazine catch lever upward until its front projection is clear of its hole in the frame, and push the catch toward the left for removal. The catch spring is mounted on the cross-shaft of the magazine catch, and will come out with it.

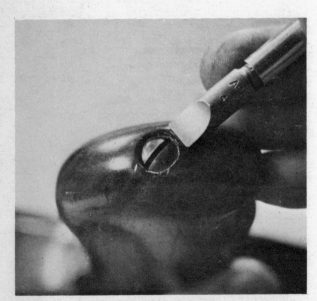

14. The rear hand grip is retained by a large screw, and the grip is taken off downward.

15. Depress the rear tip of the buffer rod (recoil spring guide) until the inside collar can be grasped. Move the assembly forward until its rear tip is clear, then lift it outward and remove the spring and guide toward the rear. Keep the spring under control.

16. Move the bolt to the rear of the receiver, and lift it out. Move the actuator forward until the H-block is pushed outward, and remove the H-block.

17. Move the actuator back until its knob aligns with the larger opening in its track, and remove the actuator downward. Inside the receiver, there is a thin steel bracket holding twin oiler pads. In normal takedown, this is best left in place.

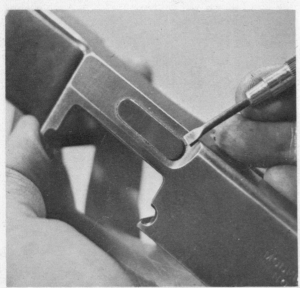

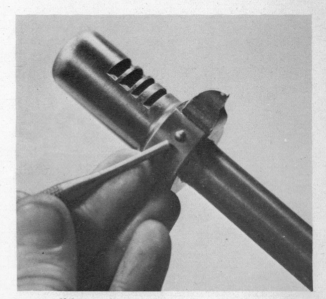

18. The ejector is removed by inserting a sharp tool to lift its rear tail until the lug is clear of its hole in the receiver, then unscrewing it, counter-clockwise (left side view). During this operation, a piece of cardboard should be used to protect the finish of the receiver from drag marks. Except for repair or refinishing, the ejector should not removed.

19. If the gun has a compensator at the muzzle, as on the one shown, drift out the cross-pin, then unscrew the compensator counter-clockwise (front view). On guns without the compensator, driving out the cross-pin will allow the front sight ring to be nudged off toward the front. The rear sight is retained by its hinge-pin, and removal will also release a plunger and spring which bear on the sight.

20. The forward hand grip is retained by a large screw, and is taken off downward.

21. The frame latch button is retained in its well by an enlarged loop at the end of its spring. Pull it out while turning the button and spring counter-clockwise (bottom view). If the button and its spring are ever jammed in the well, an access hole is provided on top of the receiver for insertion of a drift punch to nudge it out.

22. Hook a screwdriver blade under the extractor beak, as shown, and lift it just enough to clear the underlug from its well in the bolt. Then, lever the extractor toward the front for removal. In normal takedown, the extractor is best left in place.

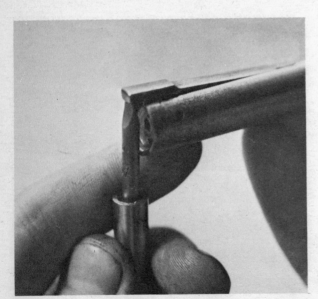

23. Push out the hammer pin toward either side.

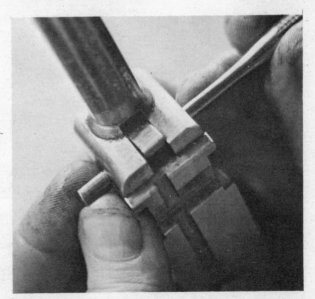

24. Remove the hammer from the bolt.

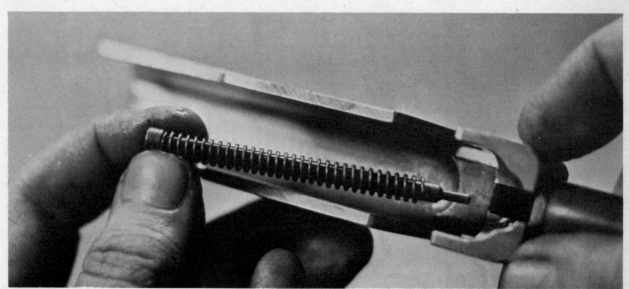

25. Remove the firing pin and its spring from the bolt.

Reassembly Tips:

1. The H-block is marked with an arrow and the word "UP" to aid reassembly. The receiver is usually inverted during disassembly and reassembly, so the "UP" marking should be visible with the receiver in that position, and the arrow should point toward the muzzle.

2. When replacing the rocker, be sure its "beak" is oriented toward the rear. If it is installed in reverse, the selector will not function, and the firing will be non-selective full-auto.

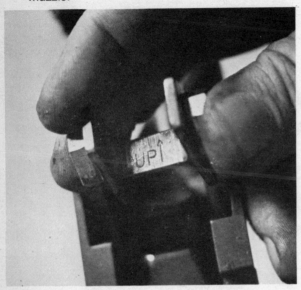

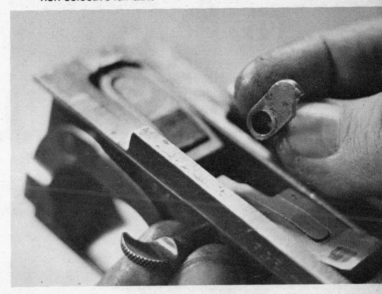

When replacing the selector ("rocker pivot") and the safety, use the leather-padded screwdriver, as in steps 4 and 5, to flex the spring arms as the parts are moved into place.

Note that the flat side of the collar on the recoil spring guide goes toward the inside top of the receiver.

U.S. M3A1

Data: U.S. M3A1
Origin: United States
Manufacturer: Guide Lamp Division
General Motors Corporation
Detroit, Michigan
Cartridge: 45 ACP
Magazine capacity: 30 rounds
Over-all length: 29.8 inches (stock extended)
Barrel length: 8 inches
Weight: 8¾ pounds

The M3A1 replaced the original M3 gun, and all other submachine guns in the U.S. service, in April, 1945. It saw little use in World War II, but its use in the Korean War prompted additional production in 1950 by Ithaca Gun Company. Nationalist China at one time also produced copies of the gun. Surplus military stocks of the M3A1 have been sold to a number of law enforcement agencies, and this is the reason for its inclusion here.

Disassembly:

1. With the bolt in the forward position and the magazine removed, depress the barrel collar detent and unscrew the barrel and collar assembly for removal toward the front. The collar is retained on the barrel by a cross-pin, and this is not removed in normal disassembly. If the gun is equipped with a flash hider, this can be removed by loosening the wing nut and slipping the flash hider off toward the front.

2. Depress and hold the stock latch, and pull the wire buttstock off toward the rear.

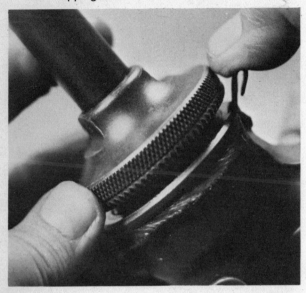

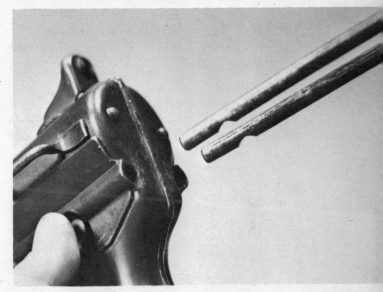

3. Insert the buttstock through the trigger guard as shown, and turn it to spring the guard out of its slot in the front of the pistol grip.

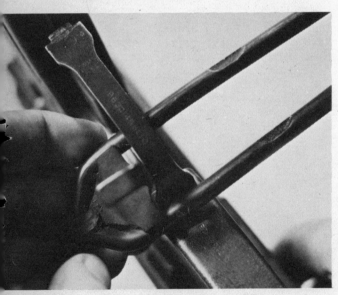

4. Tip the trigger guard over toward the front, and remove it.

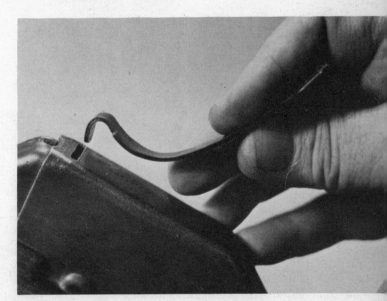

5. Tip the housing assembly downward at the rear, and remove it. The ejector is riveted to the housing, and is not removed in normal takedown.

6. Open the ejection port cover, and remove the bolt and recoil spring assembly toward the front.

7. Restrain the springs and guide rod assembly at the rear, and remove the guide rod retaining clip at the front of the guide rod locating plate. **Caution:** *Keep the springs under control.*

8. Remove the guide rod locating plate, keeping the spring system under control

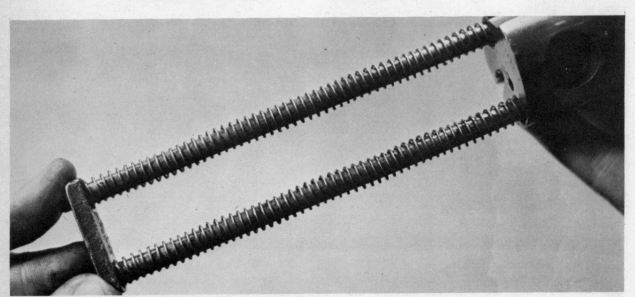

9. Release the spring tension slowly, and remove the springs and guide rod assembly toward the rear.

10. Drift out the extractor retaining pin upward.

11. If the extractor is not tightly fitted, hook a screwdriver blade under the extractor beak, and pull the extractor out toward the front. The extractor is its own spring.

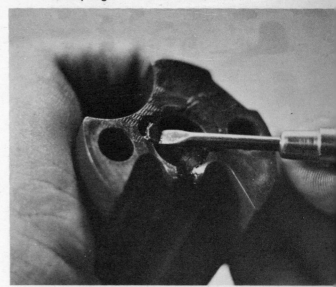

12. If the extractor is tightly fitted, insert a rod into the small hole at the rear of the bolt, and push the extractor out toward the front. This method is also used if the extractor beak is broken off.

13. Push the magazine catch cup toward the rear, off the magazine housing, and when it clears unhook the right tip of the cross-piece from its slot in the housing.

14. After the catch is removed, the cup and spring are easily separated from the catch cross-piece.

15. The ejection port cover hinge can be drifted out toward the rear to free the cover for removal. The hinge pin will usually be tightly fitted, and removal should be done only for repair.

16. Push out the sear pin toward either side. When the pin is removed, the combination trigger and sear spring will pull the sear downward, but the sear will remain attached to the trigger bar.

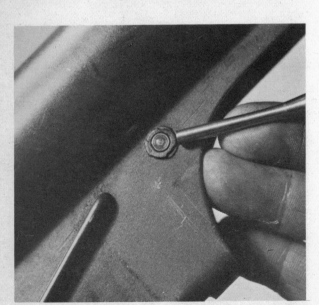

17. Remove the trigger pivot toward the right.

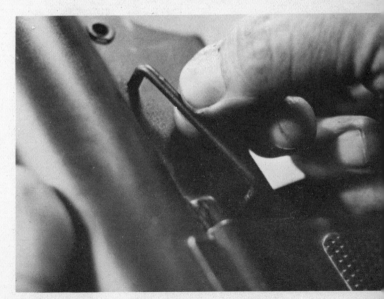

18. Move the trigger and sear assembly upward into the receiver, move the assembly forward, and take it out downward.

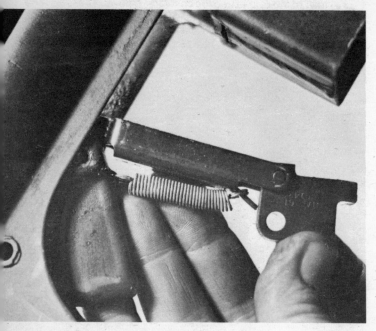

19. Push out the sear connector pin toward either side, and remove the sear from the front of the trigger bar ("connector").

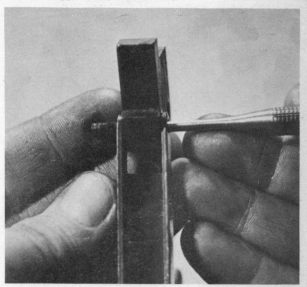

20. The combination sear and trigger spring is easily unhooked from the front of the trigger bar. The trigger bar cross-pin at the top of the trigger is semi-riveted in place, and is not routinely removed. The rear spring hook, on the front of the trigger, may be clinched, and will have to be bent outward to free the spring.

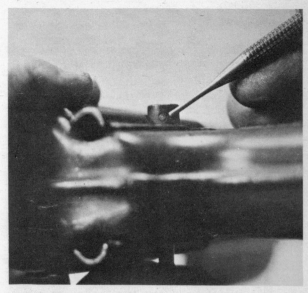

21. The stock retaining latch is retained by a collar on the right side that is cross-pinned to the latch shaft. The collar is taken off toward the right, and the latch and spring toward the left.

22. Unscrew and remove the cap and oiler rod from the oil bottle at the bottom of the pistol grip, and use a wrench of the proper size to unscrew and remove the oil bottle.

23. The barrel collar detent is retained by two rivets, and is not routinely removed.

Reassembly Tips:

1. When replacing the trigger and sear assembly, position the trigger and install the trigger pivot first. Then, elevate the sear and bar, and pull the trigger to move the sear into alignment for replacement of the sear cross-pin.

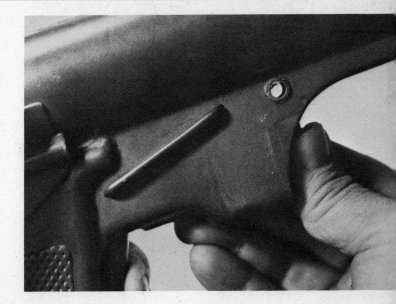

2. When replacing the bolt and spring assembly, be sure the rear tips of the guide rods snap into their holes in the rear of the receiver and protrude slightly, as shown.

3. When replacing the trigger guard, use the stock again, this time at the rear, to snap the rear tip of the guard into its slot.

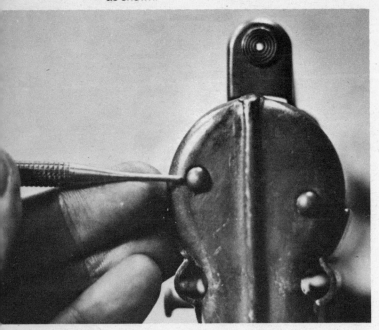

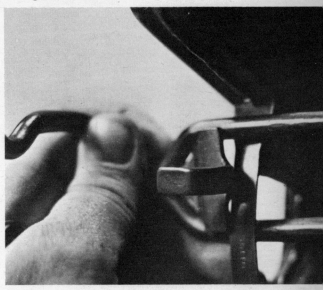